Praise for the plays of Neil LaBute

The Mercy Seat

"[A] powerful drama . . . LaBute shows a true master's hand in gliding us amid the shoals and reefs of a mined relationship."

—DONALD LYONS, *New York Post*

"Though set in the cold, gray light of morning in a downtown loft with inescapable views of the vacuum left by the twin towers, *The Mercy Seat* really occurs in one of those feverish nights of the soul in which men and women lock in vicious sexual combat, as in Strindberg's *Dance of Death* and Edward Albee's *Who's Afraid of Virginia Woolf?*" —BEN BRANTLEY, *The New York Times*

"An intelligent and thought-provoking drama that casts a less-than-glowing light on man's dark side in the face of disaster . . . The play's energy lies in LaBute's trademark scathing dialogue."

—ROBERT DOMINGUEZ, New York *Daily News*

The Shape of Things

"LaBute is the first dramatist since David Mamet and Sam Shepard—since Edward Albee, actually—to mix sympathy and savagery, pathos and power." —DONALD LYONS, *New York Post*

"LaBute . . . continues to probe the fascinating dark side of individualism . . . [His] great gift is to live in and to chronicle that murky area of not-knowing, which mankind spends much of its waking life denying." —JOHN LAHR, *The New Yorker*

"*Shape* . . . is LaBute's thesis on extreme feminine wiles, as well as a disquisition on how far an artist . . . can go in the name of art . . . Like a chiropractor of the soul, LaBute is looking for realignment, listening for a crack." —JOHN ISTEL, *Elle*

The Distance from Here

"LaBute does not trivialize darkness but treats it with proper awe . . . In his most ambitious and best play to date, [he] gets inside the emptiness of American culture, the masquerade of pleasure and the evil of neglect. *The Distance from Here* . . . is a new title to be added to the short list of important contemporary plays." —JOHN LAHR, *The New Yorker*

"A bold dramatic concept . . . [*The Distance from Here*'s] trailer trash characters are keenly observed through the fug of cigarette smoke and beer fumes that envelops their native habitat." —MARILYN STASIO, *Variety*

bash: latterday plays

"Transfixing . . . In rendering these narratives, Mr. LaBute shows not only a merciless ear for contemporary speech but also a poet's sense of recurring, slyly graduated imagery . . . Unmistakably American . . . *Bash* is informed with an earnest, probing moralism as fierce as that of Nathaniel Hawthorne." —BEN BRANTLEY, *The New York Times*

"Excellent . . . The fearsome power [of] this drama [is] meticulously crafted, so that the horror of the crimes creeps up and then slams in." —RICHARD CHRISTIANSEN, *Chicago Tribune*

"Captivating . . . LaBute's subtle poetry . . . arouse[s] a deeply disturbing emotional response." —STEVEN OXMAN, *Variety*

Ivan Kyncl

Neil LaBute

This Is How It Goes

NEIL LABUTE is a critically acclaimed playwright, filmmaker, and fiction writer. His controversial works include the plays *bash: latterday plays*, *The Distance from Here*, *The Mercy Seat* (Faber, 2003), *Fat Pig* (Faber, 2004), and *Autobahn* (Faber, 2005); the films *In the Company of Men* (Faber, 1997), *Your Friends and Neighbors* (Faber, 1998), *Nurse Betty*, and *Possession*; the play and film adaptation of *The Shape of Things* (Faber, 2001); and the short-story collection *Seconds of Pleasure*.

Other works by Neil LaBute available from Faber

In the Company of Men

Your Friends and Neighbors

The Shape of Things

The Mercy Seat

Autobahn

Fat Pig

This Is How It Goes

This Is How It Goes

A play by

Neil LaBute

FARRAR, STRAUS AND GIROUX
NEW YORK

This Is How It Goes

Farrar, Straus and Giroux

18 West 18th Street, New York 10011

Copyright © 2005 by Neil LaBute

First edition, 2005

Library of Congress Cataloging-in-Publication Data
LaBute, Neil.
This is how it goes : a play / by Neil LaBute. — 1st ed.
     p.   cm.
   ISBN-13: 978-0-571-21155-5
   ISBN-10: 0-571-21155-0 (pbk. : alk. paper)
   1. Ethnic relations—Drama.   2. Race relations—Drama.   3. Sex role—Drama.
   I. Title.

PS3612.A28T48 2005
812'.54—dc22

                                                          2004020024

Designed by Gretchen Achilles

www.fsgbooks.com

P1

For Harold Pinter

I hate the place. I hate the people.
I hate the bloody niggers.
Mustn't call 'em that, you know.

—GRAHAM GREENE

Nothing fuels a good flirtation
Like need and anger and desperation.

—AIMEE MANN

I keep a close watch on this heart of mine,
I keep my eyes wide open all the time.

—JOHNNY CASH

This Is How It Went

I'm not sure where this one came from. This is one of those plays that just sort of dropped out onto the page and I figure it's best not to ask too many questions; it's here now, so we'll just have to live with it.

I started with the title this time, I know that much. *This Is How It Goes.* I had been listening to Aimee Mann a lot before I started writing, and I can remember seeing that title on her *Lost in Space* CD and knowing, almost instantly, that I wanted to use it. It wasn't the specifics of the song itself, the lyrics or anything like that, that attracted me to it, but the implied promise of a truth revealed—knowing full well just how subjective truth can be—and the gorgeous plaintiveness of the music. Ms. Mann's work can be very inspiring. So, I took the name and ran with it. Not that I knew where I was headed, mind you, not at all, but that's rarely stopped me before. No, I simply threw two characters together—as I often enjoy doing—at a Sears in an outlet mall (I had a long history with that department store chain in my youth) and waited to see what happened. Out of that impulse grew a third character—in this case, someone who was both husband and friend—and with him a meditation on truth (the many versions of it that we offer up to different people) and some notion about how racism still affects all of us on a simple, daily level. In fact, during those initial fifteen pages or so of the first scene, I don't think I had any idea that I was going to create a "mixed" marriage—sometimes these things just sneak up on you as a writer and present themselves. Pretty diverse ingredients, I'll admit, but that's how this particular play began. I promise.

I sprinkled a number of Ms. Mann's lyrics throughout the piece, punctuating the action and dialogue with many of her clever turns of phrase—although hopefully not so many that I owe her any royalties! Again, it wasn't that any specific moment or title spoke directly to the action, but rather I used them more as a tribute to her and her work, a way of saying, "Yes, I'm out here and I'm listening." As a songwriter, Ms. Mann has a particularly acute insight into human foibles and I thank her for that. Plus, she sings so damn beautifully that it made the hours pass quickly when I had her music playing in the background. If you want, go searching for the passages yourself; they're easy enough to find. Even if you don't though, please note how deeply her voice and spirit have seeped into the fabric of this work. It's true.

I dedicated the play itself to Harold Pinter because, besides being a terrific writer and director, he continues to inspire me by his fearless examination of men and women while searching for answers, hoping for change, raging for equality—but never ducking for cover. Who can ask for more? What I really admire about Mr. Pinter's work—and strive for in my own—is that the point of it is not merely to upset people, but that what's being addressed is worth getting upset over. His numerous plays and screenplays have also been extremely instrumental in teaching me a thing or two about structure, along with the cardinal rule of writing (and cocktail parties): be interesting rather than well liked. Achieving both would be great, of course, but if you can only choose one, go for the former.

With *This Is How It Goes* I continue to dissect small communities in the Midwest, mostly because I know the territory, the people, and the mind-set. I appreciate the quality of life while remaining suspicious of the notion that everything is better in a small town. Often everything is just smaller, not better. After all, it's hard to appreciate diversity in a controlled environment, but maybe that's a role that the theater can continue to foster for itself—as an oracle of truth, no matter the size or location of the given venue. I honestly hope so. I suppose it's ironic that we must gather together in the dark around a little stage to hear the truth rather than tell each other face to face on our front lawns, but that is how it goes. No pun intended.

I also quote from Graham Greene and Johnny Cash at the beginning of this volume for good reason—each man, in his own manner, is a serious chronicler of the heart and moves me in various and profound ways. I myself am as unreliable as my own narrator when it comes to matters of that particular muscle and so I continue to work, continue to search, continue to hope. As the writer of this particular play, I utilized everything I could get my hands on to help tell the truth or at least one side of it—the shifting sands of a narrator's voice, the repetition of scenes from different perspectives, a set of stage directions that has more asides than a borsht belt comedian. Hey, whatever works. Regardless of my literary instincts, I've always found it much easier to mean well than to do well—like the main character of *This Is How It Goes*, I do my best to be a good person, but I'm completely at ease with being "pretty good." Or not. Maybe all of this is just crap and I'm alone somewhere, cackling into my soup. Who knows? That's for you to figure out. Besides, the worst offense a writer of fiction can precipitate on his unsuspecting readers is this old chestnut: "Trust me." I mean, where's the fun in that?

This Is How It Goes

This Is How It Goes had its world premiere on March 27, 2004, at the Public Theater in New York City. Director: George C. Wolfe. Executive director: Mara Manus. Managing director: Michael Hurst. Scenic design: Riccardo Hernández; costume design: Sandra Hernandez; lighting design: David Weiner; sound design: Fitz Patton; projection design: Batwin + Robin Productions. Production stage manager: Rick Steiger; stage manager: Gwen Gilliam. Casting: Jordan Thaler and Heidi Griffiths. Producer: George C. Wolfe; associate producers: Peter DuBois and Steven Tabakin.

The cast was as follows:

MAN: Ben Stiller

WOMAN: Amanda Peet

CODY: Jeffrey Wright

Characters

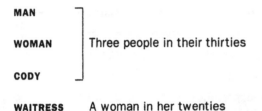

MAN

WOMAN Three people in their thirties

CODY

WAITRESS A woman in her twenties

Setting

Yesterday—a smallish town in the Midwest

NOTE: The text that follows represents the script used as the play went into rehearsals for the New York production.

Silence. Darkness.

A MAN *walks onstage. Let's give him a little light. There, that's
better. Now what? Wait—I think he's going to say something.
Yes, he is. Good.*

MAN . . . okay. This is how it goes. I mean, went. This is the
   way it all played out, or is going to. Or *is* . . . right now.
   Doesn't matter, you'll figure it out. I think. No, you will . . .
   sure you will! No problem. (*Beat.*) What you need to know for
   now, I mean, *right* at this moment, is that there was a girl.
   'Course there always is, isn't there? I mean, unless there
   isn't. Then there's not . . . but that's pretty self-explanatory.
   In this one, there's a girl. There's *definitely* a girl.

Another light up. We need it—a WOMAN *has just appeared.
Sitting all alone. For now. The* MAN *glances at her.*

MAN Huh. I think I'm gonna go talk to her, because . . . well,
   girls are nice. Basically. And that would be enough, but I
   need to—*talk* with her, I mean. To get this started. Or keep
   it going . . . or whatever. You know what I'm saying! Sort of.
   And which is okay, because *I* only sort of know, too, at this
   point. (*Beat.*) Geez, I think I might end up being an
   unreliable narrator here . . .

The MAN *starts to approach the* WOMAN, *who is seated on a bench. Moves next to her.*

MAN . . . hello.

The WOMAN *doesn't react, and the* MAN *snaps his fingers, jumping back to his light spot. What's up? Let's find out.*

MAN Just one other thing . . . I know her. From before. Like, before *now.* So, whether this is happening or, umm, has happened, is all in my head—*however* that works out—I know her already. From school. Okay? Good . . . I just wanted you to know.

The MAN *moves back over to the* WOMAN. *Taps her on the shoulder.*

MAN . . . hello.

The WOMAN *turns, looks at him. It takes a moment, then she reacts. A lot. She even stands up.*

WOMAN Yes? (*Beat.*) Oh my God . . . oh-my-God! Hey, hello. Hi!
MAN Hello. Again.
WOMAN Yeah, *again!* Way-way-back again. Wow. Hi!

Out of nowhere, a hug. Nice. Now we're getting somewhere. The MAN *hugs her right back. Of course.*

Neil LaBute

MAN I just . . . saw you. Saw you sitting there and thought, "Hey." I mean, more than that, more than just "Hey," but that was first. "Hey." You know? "I know her."

WOMAN Well, good. God, I hope it was more than that!

MAN No, it was, yeah, it totally was!

WOMAN Good, because I can't believe it! I can't believe you're just . . . I mean, standing there. *Right* outside of . . .

MAN . . . Sears. I know, funny, right?

WOMAN No, more than! It's weird . . . after, what, like, ten years? To see . . .

MAN It's twelve. Yeah. Almost twelve years.

The WOMAN *looks at him again. We might need more light now—some "Sears" light. She gives him another hug.*

WOMAN Wow. Really? It's just . . . wow. About twelve *years.*

MAN Yep. A dozen of 'em.

WOMAN That's . . . kinda weird.

MAN Yeah, but not *so* weird, right? Not like we knew each other *super* well or anything . . .

They stand looking at each other for a moment. A voice on the mall intercom interrupts them. They look up, waiting. Then talk again.

MAN . . . I just mean . . . it's okay, too, isn't it? To meet again.

WOMAN Oh, God, of course, yes. It's good! It is. It's fantastic, but, you know . . . yeah. It is weird.

MAN Uh-huh. It definitely has a "weird" flavor. There's a little *weirdness* sprinkled in there . . .

They stop again for a second, looking at each other. That's okay—give 'em some time.

WOMAN . . . you look so . . . I dunno.

MAN Different?

WOMAN No, not so much different, 'cause I could recognize you, like, almost instantly. But you're, I dunno . . .

MAN What?

WOMAN Kind of . . . I mean, you were a lot . . .

MAN I was bigger.

WOMAN . . . yes. You were a bigger guy then. In high school.

MAN I know. I was, wasn't I? Yep. *Big* boy back then!

They laugh—what the hell, let's have another hug.

MAN I did some . . . well, I did ROTC in college, and that was cool. And then, I dunno, I just sort of stopped acting like 7-Eleven was my *kitchen!*

WOMAN Right . . . right! You always used to, at lunch, you'd walk down and get those hot dogs, the—

MAN Two-for-a-dollar ones, exactly! I was, like, you know . . . that little kid at the movies, remember? The commercial at the drive-in . . . (*He demonstrates.*) "Two-fisted style!"

WOMAN I remember that . . . yes!

MAN Yeah, it was always right after the dancing candy and soda pop one . . . (*Beat.*) I mean . . . I think we even went to the movies once, there at the outdoor place that one time. Didn't we?

WOMAN . . . did we?

MAN Yeah, I think. Remember? Over at the . . . with the paddle-wheel ship out front—what was that called? The . . .

Neil LaBute

WOMAN . . . Showboat?

MAN Yes! That's it . . . some crazy double feature that we all
went to. This *group* of us. You don't recall that?

WOMAN Ummmm, no, I do . . . I think I do.

The WOMAN *stops, working to remember this. The* MAN *steps
away for a minute. Toward us.*

MAN . . . I don't think she does. Not really. I mean, she may
say she can, remember us going there, but I don't believe it.
Girls generally go on more dates and stuff than us guys do
at that age, sixteen or so, and that's probably why it's
harder to dredge up specific memories. That might be it.
'Cause it really is like yesterday for me. Seriously. It is . . .

The MAN *walks back over to her—she's still thinking. Looks
kind of lost while she does this.*

WOMAN Yeah, I think I do, actually. Yes. It was, like, a *comedy*
or some . . . wasn't it?

MAN Ahh, it was, no. It was *Dances with Wolves*, I think. And
then another one . . .

WOMAN Oh . . . (*frowns*) Well, that had some funny parts . . .
didn't it?

MAN A couple. Maybe the other one was a comedy, I don't
remember.

WOMAN Yeah, that could be it.

MAN Right, sure . . . (*Beat.*) So, is that place still open?

WOMAN What . . . the Showboat?

MAN Yeah.

WOMAN Oh, no . . . no way! There's, like, a *mall* there now or something. Strip mall—where they have stores but you walk outside. Is that what they call 'em?

MAN Uh-huh. I think so . . . I mean, sometimes they come up with a fancier name—Oakbrook Commons or whatnot—but that's basically what they are. *Strip* malls. This long "strip" of stores . . .

WOMAN Huh. Well, that was maybe eight years ago they did that. Put in the strip there. (*Beat.*) How long since you've been back?

MAN Oh, you know . . .

WOMAN Umm, no, not really.

MAN No, I mean, I wasn't finished . . . sorry. I guess, around, ahh, maybe five years. Well, one time about three months ago, just out at the airport—missed a connection, so I was there for a couple hours—but five years, more or less.

WOMAN . . . wow. (*smiles*) Hmmm.

MAN What? What's so funny?

WOMAN That was a *lot* of answer for, you know, that one question.

MAN Sorry! God, yeah, I can go on a little bit . . .

WOMAN No, don't be . . .

MAN I guess I'm kinda *thorough* . . . it's the law school in me.

WOMAN Oh . . . great! So, you're, I mean . . . is that your job? "Lawyer"?

MAN No . . . 'fraid not. That's my ex-job. *Ex*-lawyer. *Ex*-husband, *ex*-military. (*Beat.*) I'm great at "used to be."

The WOMAN *laughs at this. An easy laugh. She's loosening up a bit. That's nice.*

Neil LaBute

WOMAN That's funny . . . I remember now. You were always
pretty funny.

MAN Yeah? Good. Glad you thought that.

WOMAN Oh, yeah . . . *every*body thought you were funny.

MAN Yep . . . that's me. *Mr.* Comedy. (*Beat.*) Anyhow, sorry
about going on like that before . . . blah-blah-blah!

WOMAN No, I wasn't saying . . . I mean, it's nice.

MAN Yeah?

WOMAN To talk, I mean. About, you know . . . whatever. Just
have a five-minute *conversation* with a person . . .

MAN Why, is your husband a mute?

The WOMAN *looks at him strangely for a moment, without
speaking. The* MAN *clears his throat.*

MAN I just . . . God, I hope not! I was kidding. I saw your ring,
noticed it, and . . . that's all. (*Beat.*) He *can* speak, can't
he?

WOMAN . . . rumor has it. Not to *me*, of course, but I know he
must. Every so often . . .

MAN Ahh. One of those, huh?

WOMAN Yep. He's a classic. Classic *guy* . . .

MAN Ouch. From all of us.

WOMAN No, sorry, I didn't mean . . . gosh, listen to me! Listen
to me go on like one of those people that you run into . . .
at, like . . .

MAN . . . Sears.

WOMAN Exactly!

The WOMAN *laughs again—it's a good sound. Then another hug.*

MAN People're gonna start to talk . . .

WOMAN That's okay. Let 'em! Haven't seen you in ten years, so let them say stuff if they want to . . .

MAN Twelve. It was twelve years.

WOMAN Right. Even better . . .

The WOMAN *lets this thought hang, glancing at her watch. She reacts.*

WOMAN Oh, damn . . . can you hold on a sec? I need to . . . I'm getting a couple keys cut, I need to grab them before five. Just one minute . . .

Before the MAN *can respond, the* WOMAN *scurries off. Just disappears. Let's leave the lights up for a bit. I think she'll be back—I think we can trust her.*

MAN . . . how great is that? Huh? I came in here for the *baseball card shop*, and I run into her. That's pretty damn nice, I mean . . . am I being too obvious? 'Cause I really liked her back in school, junior year—hell, even as a senior, she was in my honors English class. And civics, too, I think. Yeah. God, she was something else . . . (*remembering*) I used to sit there and watch her, watch her lips moving as she read along with the teacher when we were doing *The Scarlet Letter.* (*Beat.*) I know she's married and all, probably got kids, even, but . . . hey, I'm just saying. Whatever. 'S just a little history.

And then the WOMAN *returns. I told you she would. A small envelope of keys in one hand.*

WOMAN . . . hi. Sorry about that.

MAN Not a problem. (*points*) You lock yourself out or something?

WOMAN What, these? No . . . it's for a, we have an apartment. Over the garage. A *garage* apartment . . . you know what I mean?

MAN Ummm . . . like, an apartment that's above your garage?

WOMAN Sorry! Yes . . . now look who's being thorough! And *obvious* . . .

MAN Right! Thought I was bad . . .

WOMAN Uh-huh. Forgive me . . . comes from being around a two-year-old.

MAN Yours?

WOMAN Of course . . . a boy.

MAN No, I didn't mean like you *stole* him or anything, just . . . you could be a teacher, for all I know.

WOMAN Well, that's true. I'm not, but I could be . . . could've been a *lot* of things, but I'm the mother of a great little two-year-old.

MAN . . . plus, a wife.

WOMAN Yeah. That, too.

MAN *And* married a mute! Not many people can claim that . . .

That laugh again from the WOMAN. *The* MAN *laughs, too. Lots of laughs from these two.*

WOMAN No, guess not! Not very loudly, anyway . . . (*Beat.*) Get it? If I was mute, I couldn't . . . forget it.

MAN I never said you were mute.

WOMAN That's true. Sorry.

MAN I said you *married* a mute . . . as far as I'm concerned, you're perfect.

Big pause right here—some cards have just been thrown on the table. The WOMAN *is about to respond, thinks better of it, then looks in the little envelope and counts her keys.*

WOMAN Anyway . . . we've got this thing, this *space* over the second garage, and we fixed it up. To rent.

MAN . . . nice. Yeah, I'm looking for a place myself. (*Beat.*) So . . . two garages, huh?

WOMAN Uh-huh. He calls it a *guest house*, but it's really just a bonus room that we . . . Anyway, it's nice.

MAN Sounds good. I mean . . . complicated.

WOMAN Yeah, my husband just up and . . . hey, whatever. It'll be fine. (*Beat.*) So, it was great to see you.

MAN You, too. Seriously.

WOMAN Yeah, definitely. It definitely was . . .

MAN Well, good. Yeah. So . . . take care.

WOMAN And you, too! Yeah, you should as well. Ummm . . .

MAN Okay. O-kay. (*Beat.*) So, maybe I'll see you at the *strip mall*, or . . .

WOMAN . . . I'm hardly ever over that way.

MAN I was kidding.

WOMAN Oh. All right. Because . . . no, I just thought that'd be nice. To see you again. At the Wal-Mart there, or . . .

MAN . . . Shoe Carnival . . .

WOMAN Exactly! That would make me happy. To do that. And there's one of those over there, too, so . . .

MAN Well, we're damn near *obligated*, then, aren't we? (*laughs*) I mean, we could . . . we can make that happen, I

suppose. A strip mall *rendezvous*. (*Beat*.) I'm generally
pretty free in the daytime . . .

WOMAN So, later'd be bad? Just so I know, because . . .

MAN No, I was gonna say, followed by evenings *full* of nothing
to do. My nights, of course, are absolutely open . . .

*An ease between them is starting to build. It feels nice, even
from way over here. Comfortable.*

WOMAN I can always get a sitter. If I need to. My mom or
whomever . . .

MAN No, we don't have to make it too late . . . whatever works
for you.

WOMAN Or my husband could watch him. Cody.

MAN That's cute. Isn't that a really popular kid's name? Cody.

WOMAN I guess so, but no, that's, no . . . my son's name is
Ralph. Cody's his dad. That's *his* name . . .

MAN Huh. Ralph. Well, equally sweet.

WOMAN Not really, come on . . . be honest.

MAN Seriously?

WOMAN Sure, why not? People should be honest with each
other . . . every twelve years or so.

MAN Okay, good . . . that's really hideous. For a child, I mean.

WOMAN Yeah, I know. (*Beat*.) It's his dad's name. *Middle* name,
really. One of those family thingies, you know . . .

MAN . . . in which you had no say.

WOMAN You must be a great lawyer.

MAN *Ex*-lawyer.

WOMAN Right . . .

MAN . . . and I was only fair at it. Just average. (*Beat*.) The
Ralph thing was kinda easy.

This Is How It Goes

WOMAN Really?

MAN Yeah . . . I mean, with a dad named Cody.

WOMAN Well, what can you expect from a *mute*, right?

This time it's the MAN *who laughs first. Quite happily. I'm starting to have high hopes for these two.*

MAN . . . I knew a Cody in school. Our school. That guy who ran track . . . the runner.

WOMAN Me, too. I mean . . . still do.

The MAN *stops in his tracks—well, he's not really moving, but if he were, he'd be stopped in his tracks. He processes.*

MAN . . . oh. That's right, I remember you guys were . . . so, you *married* Cody Phipps?

WOMAN That's me . . .

MAN Belinda *Phipps*. Huh. Geez.

WOMAN Wow . . . you pronounce it like a death sentence.

MAN Is it?

WOMAN Umm, no, not really . . . it's probably pretty regular. As marriages go.

MAN Great . . .

WOMAN . . . didn't say it was that. No, it's just . . .

MAN . . . regular.

WOMAN Yep.

MAN Cody Phipps. That's . . . wild.

WOMAN Why? (*a bit defensive*) How so?

MAN Just, you know . . . I dunno. Well, he was a talker, for one thing. In, like, gym . . . you couldn't shut the guy up! So, when you said . . .

WOMAN Yeah, well, he got a lot quieter . . .

MAN Huh. I guess we all do, though. People tend to, in life . . .

WOMAN Uh-huh. He got a *lot* a lot quieter.

MAN I see. (*checks watch*) Hey, you know what? I need to, umm . . .

WOMAN God, I'm sorry, *listen* to me . . . who cares, right?

MAN No, it's not that, promise. (*Beat.*) I have to pick up some dry cleaning in a minute, that's all . . . I've got an interview or two this week, so I need . . .

WOMAN 'Kay. Anyway . . . great to see you.

MAN You, too. Honestly. You look—

WOMAN Don't say it! It'll never be right.

MAN Okay. But you do . . . seriously.

WOMAN Thank you. You, too.

MAN . . . so, Shoe Carnival it is, then?

WOMAN Absolutely! When?

MAN Anytime.

WOMAN Ahhh, this week. (*Beat.*) Ralph needs some new sandals . . .

MAN Got it. How about tomorrow, one-thirty?

WOMAN Great! Okay then . . . bye.

MAN Bye. And say hi to, you know . . .

WOMAN "Flyin' " Cody Phipps . . .

MAN Yep. That's the guy!

WOMAN I will. See you . . .

MAN Goodbye, *Mrs.* Phipps . . .

A last hug—and it's a nice one. The WOMAN *is gone, and those Sears lights fade. The* MAN *wanders back to his first spot.*

MAN Cody Phipps. Ho-ly shit . . . I mean, you know, come on.
Come on! I can't believe she went and . . . no, that's not
true. I guess you can believe whatever happens in life—
there's actually very little that is *unbelievable*. And I'd heard
that they were . . . but that's way out there. Cody Phipps.
Not that he wasn't, you know, popular and stuff, or good-
looking, that type of thing . . . and that dude could run!
Damn, could he . . . He was amazing. Not fast, not so much
that, like a lotta those guys are . . . he didn't *sprint* or
anything. No, Cody did all the distances. He would kill you in
the long haul, just totally wear you down, then fly right past
you . . . 800. 1,200. The 1,500. Cross-country in the fall,
which sorta pissed people off because he was great at
football, too, but nothing he liked more than running. (*Beat.*)
Suppose he still is . . . a runner, I mean. When you like
something, a sport, or do a pastime like that, you hardly
ever just give it up. Forget about it.

*The lights change to some sort of restaurant. Now there are a
table and some chairs—I didn't even notice them before.*

MAN Why don't we just go meet the guy? Save a little time.
You know, I could talk all night or however long we're gonna
be here about Cody Phipps—longer about Belinda—but if we
were to meet him, just take a second and get acquainted . . .
I think it'd start to help pull this thing all together for you.
Okay? Cool . . .

*The MAN walks over to one of the chairs, sits. Not long after
ANOTHER MAN walks in. About the same age. A black guy. He
motions toward a WAITRESS in the distance.*

MAN . . . hello, Cody. (*signals*) Cody?

CODY Right. Hey, how's it going? Nice to see you. Belinda's coming.

MAN Good, 'cause I was gonna—

CODY I mean, she's *right* behind me.

MAN Great.

And like the MAN *says, here she comes.* BELINDA. *Looking nice, even better than before. More put together. A smile for both men. The marrieds sit down together.*

CODY . . . so. Hey.

MAN Yeah, hello. Again.

WOMAN Hi. Glad the timing all worked out for us to . . . (*to* CODY) I told you he looks different. Doesn't he?

CODY I guess. I don't really remember you that much. I mean, from class.

MAN Thanks.

CODY No, man, no offense, I just don't. Not anybody from then, really, even though we still live here . . .

MAN That's all right. 'S the privilege of being rich . . .

CODY *smiles at this—an easy smile. He doesn't mind being called that. Some things he doesn't like, but this is okay.*

CODY Nah, hey, we're not *rich*, we just, you know . . . take advantage of the ignorant middle class, that's all! (*Beat.*) 'S true . . . take away all the Ralph Lauren and shit, they'd only be hardware stores.

WOMAN . . . comfortable. That's what we are.

MAN Huh. Anyhow, I do look different.

WOMAN You really do.

CODY You're not so fat, right?

Silence. Then the MAN *bursts out laughing—the* WOMAN *turns white. Whiter than she already is.*

WOMAN Cody . . .

CODY What? That's it, isn't it? What's the matter with the truth?

MAN No, you're right, that's pretty much it. I was fatter.

CODY 'S my point. No big deal.

MAN Very true. (*to the* WOMAN) I thought you said the guy didn't talk much.

Another silence. The MAN *means it as a joke, but it obviously stings. The marrieds glance at each other.*

WOMAN I just meant that . . . you know . . .

CODY You say that?

WOMAN I wasn't . . . we were talking about school and all, and I . . .

CODY Shit. (*to the* MAN) I talk. I just don't *over*talk . . .

MAN Got it. See, now, this is the Cody I remember. He always had *plenty* to say . . .

CODY Still do, man. I always do. Just say it in my own time . . .

On that, CODY *raises a hand to try and catch the eye of the passing* WAITRESS. *She doesn't even pause.* CODY *nods, turns back to the others.*

Neil LaBute

CODY . . . somebody else might as well try it, 'cause she ain't coming over here for *me*. (*Beat*.) Doesn't matter how many shops I open in the area, I'm flat outta luck when it comes to gettin' some *service* . . .

WOMAN Honey, I don't think she saw you.

CODY 'Course she did. She totally saw me. My hand in the air, like a *schoolboy* or something . . .

MAN Nah . . . I think this place always had bad service.

CODY Yeah? When'd you eat here last?

MAN Good point. A *decade* or so . . .

WOMAN It's okay, I can . . .

The WOMAN *starts to stand, gets to her feet even, before* CODY *places a hand on her wrist. A firm hand.*

CODY: Just sit. You don't have to do that, go begging . . .

WOMAN I'm not, I'm just going to . . .

CODY *Sit*. Jesus, just when she comes by again, keep an eye out. Okay?

WOMAN Sure.

The WOMAN *sits again. Settles herself. A quick glance over at the* MAN.

MAN I can go order us all something at the bar, if you guys want . . .

CODY No need. She'll be back . . . (*smiles*) That's the thing about women, they always come back. Mostly.

MAN That's a lovely sentiment . . .

CODY What?

MAN . . . nothing. I was kidding.

CODY I wasn't being sentimental. It's true, is all. Women do all kinds of shit, but they usually come back.

WOMAN Honey, why don't we . . . ?

MAN Like Lassie, you mean?

CODY Huh?

MAN Sorry. Another joke . . . Lassie was famous for getting home. Returning. I think they even made a movie of it. *Lassie Come Home* or something. And she was a woman . . . or female dog, anyway.

CODY . . . a bitch.

MAN Well, yeah, technically.

WOMAN Sweetie . . .

CODY What? That's what they're called.

WOMAN I know, but . . . people are . . .

CODY It's just a word. What's wrong with that? Words only have power if you let 'em . . .

MAN Good point. Right.

The WAITRESS *is moving past again. The* MAN *practically stands up to get her attention. She stops at the table.*

MAN . . . hi there. Hey. Could we get, umm, well, just a Coke for me, no ice. And . . . ?

WOMAN I'd take a lemonade, if that's okay.

CODY 'Course it's okay, we're gonna pay for it, aren't we? (*to* WAITRESS) And now that you're *here* . . . water.

She nods and wanders off toward the kitchen. Well, backstage, actually, but we'll pretend there's a kitchen.

Neil LaBute

MAN . . . I think you made a friend.

CODY Shit . . .

WOMAN That's all Cody drinks is water. Ever since I've known him.

MAN Yeah?

CODY Pretty much. 'S good stuff. "Pure. Clean. Feeds the machine." That's what my dad told me, anyway . . .

MAN . . . and it rhymes, which is cool.

CODY You're kind of a smart-ass, aren't ya? Like, a *jokester*.

MAN Just a little bit.

CODY I think I do remember you now. We had P.E. together or something . . . traded a few rookie cards once.

MAN Yep. That's right.

CODY You could play a little dodgeball, but that was about it . . .

MAN And "a little" would be stretching it.

CODY You were okay, for a big kid. Hard as shit to hit, most times . . .

MAN . . . it was just fear. Purely fear.

CODY 'S a good game, dodgeball. Yeah.

WOMAN We never played it . . . I mean, over on the girls' side of the gym. I think we did a gymnastics unit at that point, or maybe volleyball . . .

MAN Huh.

A silence seeps into the proceedings. Smiles between the MAN *and* WOMAN. CODY *looks around for the drinks.*

MAN . . . so, Cody, you still a runner?

CODY Yep. Every day.

MAN Great.

WOMAN Ten miles . . .

CODY Not always. Sometimes I gotta get into the office early, but usually I can burn up ten by breakfast.

MAN Wow. That's . . . I mean, I started jogging a little, in the service, but you know, like, two, maybe two and a half's all.

CODY Hardly break a sweat like that! Not even burning calories till around forty-five minutes . . .

MAN Yeah, but I just do it for fun.

CODY *Fun?*

MAN Sort of. Got hooked on it . . . (*Beat.*) We should go sometime.

CODY . . . I don't do nothing for fun.

WOMAN Cody, come on . . . (*to the* MAN) That is not true. He's . . .

CODY What? What do I do that's fun . . . or "for" fun?

WOMAN Umm . . . oh, you know. Just stuff. All people have fun.

MAN I do.

CODY Well, then, we're different people, aren't we?

MAN That is true.

WOMAN Ahhh . . . you help out at the school. With track. That's fun, isn't it?

CODY Yeah, but it's . . . no. It's helping out. I mean, yes, I *like* it, but I don't do it for fun. I coach a few runners, that's not, like, some big *hobby* or anything . . .

MAN That's great. Give a little back . . .

CODY . . . that would imply that they gave me something in the first place.

MAN Touché.

*The two men look at each other—a smile between them. It's
one of those guy things; better just leave it be.*

WOMAN What about your golf?
CODY Please . . . that's business. I do that 'cause these
    Midwestern dudes love it, so out I go . . . once they let me
    on the course, I mean.

CODY *seems happy to pursue this subject when the* **WAITRESS**
returns, dropping off the drinks. Not a word out of her.

MAN . . . she seems very sweet.
WOMAN Right! (*laughs*) A lovely young woman.
CODY Yeah, de-light-ful.

The **MAN** *smiles at this and takes a sip. So does the* **WOMAN**.
CODY *looks around the restaurant as the* **MAN** *suddenly stands.*

MAN . . . I think this is Diet. Lemme run it up front, it'll be
    faster.
CODY Give 'em hell . . .
MAN Yep, that's me. The Hellraiser . . . (*gestures*) If my head
    was shaved, you could see the *pins* and everything! (*Beat.*)
    You know, the movie with the guy who's all . . . I'll be right
    back.

The **MAN** *smiles and moves back into his original light. Looks
out at us.*

MAN . . . I gotta be honest. That was a total line I just threw
    out there, the Diet Coke thing. Yeah. See, I thought it was

getting a little bit uncomfortable, didn't you? Uh-huh. Kind
of, anyway. So I just wanted to take a sec and regroup
here . . .

The MAN *looks back over at* CODY *and the* WOMAN. *They sit in
silence, maybe a perfunctory word or two.*

MAN Is it me, or does he seem a little pissed off? I totally get
    that vibe from him. Pissed right off about something. (*Beat.*)
    He didn't always use to be that way, not when I knew him,
    anyhow. Not that we were, like, tight or anything. Best buds.
    But I knew him enough . . . enough to say that much about
    him, and he never seemed so keyed up like this. I mean,
    maybe after his mom left, for a while there he was kinda . . .
    you know. How you get when that sort of thing happens.
    You're just cruising along and then, wham! Life gets, like, all
    shitty. Matter of minutes . . . I think that's what happened to
    him. And, thing is, she'd do it about every other *month.* Plus
    there's the whole race thing . . . not that he made a huge
    deal about it at school, but yeah, he pulled that card out a
    few times back then. Just once or twice a *day!* Nobody really
    called him on it, but it was completely obvious when he'd do
    it. School lunch line, picking teams for gym, when some girl
    or other wouldn't go out with him . . . like, *whenever* he
    needed some excuse, basically. We used to call it the ol'
    "Ace 'a Spades." I mean, not to his face, God no, you
    kidding? Cody was, well, you know . . . kinda fierce. Pretty
    serious when he wanted to be, so no. We'd say it when we
    were alone, just a few of the guys. Say, like, "Hey, Cody just
    whipped out the Ace 'a Spades." And that's when
    somebody'd say, one of my friends would . . . "Just gotta call

a spade a spade." (*smiles*) We were only just joking, but it was pretty funny. At the time . . .

The MAN *looks to us for validation—does he get any? Well, we'll have to see. For now let's imagine that it remains silent out there. He nods, then turns back toward the table.*

MAN I'm gonna head back over now . . . new drink wouldn't really take all that long to get, right?

The MAN *nods to us, then turns and moves back to his chair. Sipping from his old drink as he arrives.*

MAN . . . I was right.

CODY Yeah? Looks like the same thing . . .

MAN Well, it's a Coke glass. They all have the same kind of . . .

CODY No, the color of it. Seems a little light, like the last one did.

MAN Huh. No, it's . . .

WOMAN Does it taste okay?

MAN Yeah! Just fine, thanks . . .

WOMAN Great.

MAN 'S a classic taste, isn't it?

WOMAN Yes, I love it. The original one.

CODY I wouldn't know. Don't drink soft drinks . . . no *pop* for me.

MAN That's good.

CODY Why?

MAN Well, you know . . .

CODY No, what? It's just a choice.

MAN Yeah, but a pretty healthy one. I mean—

CODY Whatever. (*Beat.*) So . . . what brings you back to town?

MAN Umm, this and that. Stuff. How's that for vague?

CODY Pretty good. You nailed it. So?

WOMAN Cody, if he doesn't want to . . .

MAN No, I'll talk about it, that's . . . not much to "talk" about in that sense, really. I'm just moving back. I miss it.

CODY . . . yeah? You miss *this* place?

MAN I do.

CODY Huh.

WOMAN That's nice. You know? To miss the town where you . . . people don't care enough about their roots, I don't think.

MAN I agree. It's easy to forget what's important. Where you come from.

WOMAN I know, it really is. *Roots* . . .

CODY What do you mean by that?

MAN I think she's saying you should move back to Africa . . .

Big silence on this one. Remember how I said there are certain things CODY *doesn't like? This would be one of them.*

CODY . . . man, that is not cool.

MAN It's a *joke*. (*Beat.*) I mean, come on, Cody, I was just . . . "Words only have power if you let them." Right?

WOMAN Honey, I don't think he meant to—

CODY No, hey, whatever. Come to meet a guy, allow him to move into my *home*, and he insults me, that's fine. If you don't mind that, ho-ney, then that's fine . . .

MAN I didn't . . . it wasn't meant as a hurtful thing. God, no! I was just trying to be funny. (*Beat.*) Sorry.

WOMAN I think we're all just a little tense. Nervous.

CODY I'm not nervous, why would I be nervous? Hmm?

WOMAN I dunno, maybe . . . you know.

CODY No. I don't know. I've got this nice new studio over
my garage, and I'm looking for a tenant. Not some
asshole.

MAN Cody, honestly . . . forgive me. It was just a . . . she said
"roots," and it popped into my head. That's—

CODY Oh.

MAN The show, that's all. With the dad from *Good Times* and,
you know, that dancer . . . somebody Vereen. (*Beat.*) There
was no disrespect meant. It was a mistake . . .

CODY Fine.

WOMAN It's okay.

CODY Hey. (*looks at* WOMAN) Don't you do that. Don't apologize
for me, or go saying that something is okay. Got that? Do-
not. I said it was fine, not that it was okay. *Big*, big
difference . . .

WOMAN I'm sorry. Cody, please, I—

MAN What's the difference?

CODY What?

MAN No, I mean, you said something about the difference
between "fine" and "okay," and I'm trying to think what it is.

CODY Dude, just leave it.

MAN All right. Just trying to . . .

WOMAN Why don't we . . .

CODY You know what "okay" means, means that it's okay. It's
all all right. And "fine" is something else. Says, "Yeah, I'll let
it go." *I'm* letting it go. Fine. But it is not o-kay.

*They all take long, uncomfortable sips from their beverages.
The* WAITRESS *passes again. Oblivious. Doesn't see* CODY *raise
his hand.*

CODY . . . and that shit is not "okay," either! What is it with her?

MAN You got me. (*Beat.*) Do you need something?

WOMAN She's probably trying to cover too many tables . . . I used to work here back whenever, in school. (*to the men*) Do you remember that?

MAN Depends. Do you remember me sitting in that corner booth there, almost every day after school?

WOMAN . . . I do. With your homework.

MAN Yep!

CODY I never came in here. Least not back then, anyhow. And not after school. I had sports . . .

MAN Right, 'course you did.

CODY Yeah.

WOMAN It was always quiet then, around four or so, before the dinner rush . . . and you'd be over there reading and sipping on a drink.

MAN Uh-huh. And probably a basket of cheese fries, too! I was a *porker* in those days . . . God.

CODY Yep. You were kind of a tubby sorta guy then, weren't you?

MAN Oh yeah.

CODY And with the wise mouth, too.

MAN You are correct, sir.

CODY Surprised you didn't get picked on more . . . beat up and shit.

MAN I got my share, don't worry. There was plenty of that . . .

WOMAN That's awful.

MAN Nah, made me a better person. It's what I told myself, anyway, lying there in *traction* . . .

WOMAN Oh my God. (*Beat.*) Really?

CODY No, that's bullshit.

MAN 'Course it is. But I did get a few bumps in my day . . . the occasional *undies* up the flagpole.

CODY *laughs at this, the first time we've heard that. It seems out of place, almost frightening.*

MAN . . . well, now I know who was behind *that!*

CODY No, man, sorry, but, I can remember it. Seriously. Seeing your Fruit of the Looms flapping up there, all the way down by the track! Certain times . . . that was funny.

CODY *laughs halfheartedly again, but it's passed now. Over.*

CODY Anyway, whatever. So what's the deal? You want the place or not?

MAN Ummm . . .

WOMAN Honey, he'd probably like to see it first. (*to the* MAN) Right?

MAN Yeah, that'd be—

CODY Why? I mean, it's new. All the stuff in there is *new*, so what's the problem?

MAN Nothing, no, just that it's, you know . . . furnished.

CODY So?

MAN So, I'd like to see if my things'll go with . . . I dunno. The *carpet* . . .

CODY Oh. Okay, fine, if you're like *that* about it, all *particular*, then okay. Do it. Check it out.

MAN Thanks.

WOMAN It's pretty nice. We did it all in neutrals. You know, with whites and creams and that sort of—

MAN Great. I'll take a look. And it's how much . . . six-fifty?

CODY Yep. (*Beat.*) I was planning to knock it down if somebody wanted to do a little yard work for me . . .

WOMAN Cody, we never—

CODY I know, I know, I'm joking! I can *joke*, too, can't I?

MAN Sure. No, I'd make a hell of an indentured servant . . . you're right.

CODY I'm not talking about no servant. If you do some gardening, you get paid. That's all. (*to the* WOMAN) Did the same thing with that one student, the exchange student. Remember?

The WOMAN *nods, then takes a sip. Quiet for a moment. That's okay, they all need a breather.*

MAN Sure. I know, I get it. And I'm not above that . . . (*Beat.*) Beggars can't be . . . well, you know.

CODY Exactly.

MAN Great.

WOMAN Well, that's really nice . . . we can set a time to take a look later.

MAN Perfect.

CODY . . . and why're you here again? Back in town, I mean?

MAN Just, you know . . . getting back to basics. Simplifying. (*Beat.*) Wasn't so big on the corporate thing, all the wheeling and dealing I had to do, that sorta stuff. I'm no lawyer, that's what I found out. 'Course, I had to go to law school and take on about seventy *thousand* in loans to figure it out, but hey!

They all chuckle at this—kind of vacantly, but they're trying.

MAN Anyhow, I'm cutting back, gonna do some writing that I always wanted to do, and . . .

WOMAN That sounds good . . .

CODY Sort of like that Grisham, huh?

MAN What, you mean . . . John Grisham?

CODY Yeah, he did that, right? Stopped being a lawyer and became a writer.

MAN Uh-huh. Yes, like that. Except for the theater . . . I'm gonna be a—

CODY Well, that's cool . . . lawyers are pretty good at making shit up. I know *mine* are! (*laughs*) Great.

WOMAN . . . that's exciting . . .

MAN Yep. Might have to sell a bit of my card collection for cash, but . . .

CODY Yeah . . . seriously?

MAN Maybe. Thought I'd . . .

CODY You still got that Jackie Robinson you took off me? Huh?

MAN Hey, I didn't "take" it off you, you traded it . . .

CODY Yes, but . . .

MAN Fair and square. (*to the* WOMAN) Guy is still sore about that!

CODY 'S my favorite card.

MAN Then you should've kept it . . .

CODY Right.

WOMAN What is it . . . a baseball card?

MAN Uh-huh. It's one he gave me back in school. For a favor.

WOMAN Wow . . . that doesn't sound like Cody. Asking for *help* from somebody . . .

CODY Yeah, well, I needed it. (*Beat.*) It was a sweet card, too.

MAN I know. 1952 Topps. Mint condition. (*to the* WOMAN *again*) You know why there are so few Robinson cards from that time?

WOMAN Uh-uh. Why?

CODY Because people destroyed 'em. Dads, their kids, folks would get them—white folks, that is—find them in their gum pack and rip the fuck out of 'em because the dude was a black man, this uppity black who somehow snuck his way onto a ball team . . . that is why. Guys across America were tearing his picture up to show that they did not like it. Rookie of the year, MVP, they still didn't give a shit. And that's why it's so damn rare . . .

WOMAN . . . and that's why you want it?

CODY You don't get it. (*to the* MAN) She doesn't get shit like this. Never has . . .

MAN That's okay. It's pretty much a guy thing . . . (*to the* WOMAN) It's not just that, anyway. This one had a flaw in it. 'S a misprint that—

CODY Whatever. (*Beat.*) You serious about it, I'll swing a deal with you.

MAN Maybe. I'm probably gonna need to do something . . . actually, as long as I can pay the child support, I'm okay . . .

WOMAN Oh. Oh! I wasn't . . . I mean, I didn't know you had kids. That's . . . great.

MAN *Kid.* Just the one. A girl.

CODY Where's she at?

MAN My daughter? Oh, she's, you know, with her mom.

CODY Man, I could never give up my kids.

Neil LaBute

This reference is caught by the MAN—*he and the* WOMAN *should share a brief look—before he goes on.*

MAN I didn't give 'er up . . . I see her all the time. It's just . . .

CODY Complicated, I'm sure. Always is. Raising kids isn't complicated, you ain't doing it right . . . (*Beat.*) But hey, that's your business.

CODY *stands, stretches, then puts out a hand.*

CODY I gotta go, need to swing past the store over on Tamarack. Replaced a manager, so . . .

The MAN *stands, along with the* WOMAN. CODY *and his wife hold a look for a moment.*

CODY Good to see you. And look, you two work out a time to check the place and make a decision or not on the, you know, *carpet* . . . (*shakes hands with the* MAN) See ya.

MAN Yeah, you, too.

WOMAN Bye, sweetie. (*They kiss.*) Talk to you later.

CODY *nods as he drops a wad of cash on the table. Exits.*

MAN . . . well. That was . . . huh.

WOMAN Yeah. Sorry.

MAN No, totally fine, just not what I was expecting. It got a little hot there for a minute . . .

WOMAN I know. Yes.

MAN So . . . "kids," huh? You didn't say that before. *Kids.* How come?

This Is How It Goes

WOMAN Oh, you know . . . because.

MAN No, why?

WOMAN . . . because he hates me. Cody *Jr.* He's *six,* and he
pretty much hates me. (*Beat.*) I'll just pay for the . . .

The WOMAN *tries to smile but just misses pulling it off. She
grabs the money and heads to the counter. The* MAN *is alone.*

MAN . . . anyway, it was more or less like that. I'm not
completely sure she said his name then, her other son's, but
she might've. Probably did. And, so, that's how I got into the
apartment over the garage. I mean, I may've walked her out
to her car, or am going to—I still don't get the time thing
here!—but it basically happened that way. Cody all tense and
whatever, and me just trying to stay out of the way. Her, too.
Belinda, I mean. Yeah, I get the feeling that she needs to
stay out of the way a lot . . . or, as she said earlier (or will
later), a *lot* a lot. Yeah . . .

*Lights need to pop up now on another playing area—turns out
we're going to need a few. This one should be some kind of
nice sitting-room area. Just a few pieces to suggest it. We'll
fake the rest.*

MAN We should probably keep moving now. Most of you'll need
to get on home after this, right? I'm sure you do. Even if you
have no one to get home to, you still need to get there . . .
Okay, good. Now, I'm not going to be in this next bit, I mean,
I will in *spirit* or whatever, because I'll be talked about,
things like that, but I won't actually be there. Don't worry,
though, no big deal, I'm gonna be back . . . maybe just

imagine I'm up in the apartment there . . . fixing my lunch or reading some book, that kind of thing. Making notes. I may even have myself a little job by this point—I do end up helping out with the yard work—so, something along those lines. But this part right now is pretty important to the rest, so do pay attention . . . 'Kay? Fine. (*Beat.*) If you don't, you'll never find out how Belinda ends up with the black guy . . . "eye," I mean "black *eye*"! Geez, that's a Freudian slip, huh? (*chuckles*) Like I said, I wasn't there, so I didn't see it—or won't—but *you* get to see it all. If you pay attention. All I know is later, when Cody's out at the office, she comes to me, and I see it and freak out a bit, but she never actually tells me about what happened. Not really. (*Beat.*) So, this is how it goes. This part. Okay, I'll shut up now . . .

The MAN *smiles and backs off, disappearing just as the* WOMAN *enters. She plops onto the couch after putting a baby monitor down on the coffee table. Sorry—yeah, we'll need a coffee table, too. She has a magazine and a diet cola with her.*

WOMAN . . . hello? (*Beat.*) I'm in here!
CODY (*offstage*) Why? Why're you in there?
WOMAN I just . . . because.

CODY *enters, drenched in sweat from working out. Nike shirt, shorts. Maybe even wearing sunglasses. He looks pretty cool.*

CODY 'Cause why? Huh? Why do you always hole up in this room, way the other side of the house?
WOMAN Cody, I like it in here. It's sunny during the morning, and I can relax a minute when the baby's asleep . . .

CODY Hey, he's not a baby, okay? Kid is two years old . . . you *treat* him like a baby, but he's not.

WOMAN Listen, he needs to—

CODY No, you listen. What he doesn't need is taking a nap at eight in the morning! All right? He just got up, like, an hour and a half ago. And you give 'im breakfast and back to bed he goes . . . that's wrong.

WOMAN He's tired. He's—

CODY No, you're lazy, that's what it is.

WOMAN "Lazy"?

CODY You heard me. Yeah. You get Cody Jr. off to school— great—and put a little food down Ralph, and then that's it for the day, far as you think . . .

WOMAN That is not . . .

CODY Bullshit! Bull-shit. I know it is.

WOMAN Cody, our son is tired, do you mind? I know *you* don't get that way, since you run every day and never come to bed before, say, *two* in the morning . . . but other people, we sleep. He's a child. A growing boy, and he needs a nap whenever he feels like it. Right now, an hour from now . . . whenever.

CODY *shakes his head and pulls off his shirt, flexing. Does a few stretches. Yes, he's in good shape.*

CODY That shit is abuse . . .

WOMAN What?! I mean, why would you even say . . . ?

CODY It is! You ever hear of *raising* children? Huh? *You* raise them, they don't do it themselves . . . You're the parent, you set the rules, make the choices. Not the kid.

Neil LaBute

WOMAN And when was the last time you took part in that? "Raising" him. Hmm?

CODY Don't start that crap . . . *I* work.

WOMAN Oh, please . . .

CODY What?! I do, 's more than you can say.

WOMAN Cody! I mean . . .

CODY . . . hey, truth hurts.

WOMAN (*to herself*) God . . . this is like a Thomas Hardy novel or something.

CODY The fuck does that mean?

WOMAN . . . that's kinda *Victorian*, don't you think? "I work." I mean, come on . . . we both work, I just happen to work *here*. In this house of yours. I mean, your father's—

CODY It's my house. *My* house. 'Kay? He's dead and this is mine. Including this room here, which you know I hate you being in . . .

WOMAN *Why?!*

CODY Because it's a sitting room, okay? "Sitting." Supposed to be for the evening, or when you have guests over . . .

WOMAN No, it's not.

CODY Yeah, it is. Yes! You go read one of those *Architectural Digest*s or something I have in the den, it'll tell you the same damn thing . . .

WOMAN Who cares?

CODY I do. I care! You sitting in here, middle of the morning, with your feet up and sucking down that damn Tab you drink all the time . . . looks lazy. You look like a fuckin' pig, and I hate it!

WOMAN Wow. Okay, that's . . . well, that's a new one. I mean, you've usually got something *lousy* to say to me, but that there is a completely new one. Congratulations . . .

CODY Shut up.

WOMAN Nice comeback . . .

CODY Fuck that. I don't need a *comeback*. I need a wife who doesn't park it on her fat ass all day, sucking on pop like she's some sixteen-year-old . . .

WOMAN I wish I was.

CODY What?

WOMAN That. Sixteen . . .

CODY Yeah, why's that?

WOMAN . . . because that was the year *before* I met you. Okay? That's why . . .

She can see CODY *react at this, but she can't stop now. Not very wise, maybe, but that's how it goes sometimes.*

CODY . . . well, well.

WOMAN Co-dy . . . I'm just saying . . . (*thinks*) I always liked you because you were different, you know? Back whenever. But now, I mean, now you're just so worried about somebody giving you shit, or disrespecting you, or I don't know what . . . and it's not about that. Black or white or any of that crap. It's about being a good guy, Cody. A *decent* person. And you're not . . . in the end, I'm with somebody who's like all the other guys I grew up around. Not so terrible, but not very good, either. You're just a guy. Just a *normal* guy . . . which means kind of shitty, actually. Completely average and a little bit shitty.

CODY *tenses up, turns to her. He starts to advance slowly, wrapping his shirt around his hand—like a boxer wraps tape around his fist before putting it in the glove. The* WOMAN *stands, facing him.*

CODY 'S that right?

WOMAN Cody, look . . . I didn't mean . . .

CODY Is it? Great. That's really great.

WOMAN . . . I wasn't being . . . don't . . .

CODY No, that's funny. You're getting real cute with your mouth lately. Must be your little friend over the garage there, making you all clever and smarty-pants like that . . .

WOMAN He hasn't been . . . no. I was just trying to say that—

CODY . . . make another wish. Go ahead . . . one more.

CODY *continues to move toward her as she backs away. Finally, she comes up against a love seat and is trapped. She looks at him, shit scared. I mean, come on, wouldn't you be? She tries to reach out and touch him.* CODY *pulls back. The* WOMAN *is starting to cry. Shaking her head.*

CODY Go on . . . make one.

WOMAN . . . I wish . . . you wouldn't hurt me.

CODY Huh. (*Beat.*) Too late . . .

CODY *smacks her flat in the stomach, doubling her over. She drops to her knees and disappears behind the small couch.*

He reaches down and hits her again, this time in the face. We can't see exactly what happens, but the sound is sickening.

For a moment, silence. Then the sound of a child waking up on the baby monitor. CODY *unwraps his hand and starts off.*

CODY I'll get 'im. (*Beat.*) You better put something on that eye. Try your *soda pop* there . . . that's nice and cold.

CODY *exits. The room is empty, the* WOMAN *still behind the piece of furniture. After a moment, the* MAN *enters the room. What's he doing here again?*

MAN . . . okay, so maybe it wasn't *exactly* like that. I dunno. Hey, look, I'm a writer—would-be writer, anyway—so, what can I tell ya? I've got a hell of an imagination, and I just go with it sometimes . . . listen, it could've happened that way! Easily—I mean, she did get the eye once, this black eye, and so, I'm just guessing. That's all. Actually . . . it's probably how I *want* it to be, like, so I can jump in there, save her or whatever. That's probably it . . . but still, this might've been a touch of an exaggeration. Yeah. Anyway, all stories need some sort of antagonist, don't they? Sure. Someone to dislike, or you want to see fail or whatever . . . well, I figure I'm gonna have to play the ol' Ace 'a Spades on that one! Yep. Only choice I've got . . . I mean, it can't be me. And not her, I don't want it to be her, so . . . Cody's the guy. (*Beat.*) But to be fair, I have no idea if it happened that way or not. The bruise thingie. No . . . that was probably a bit much, we should go ahead and give it another try.

Suddenly, the WOMAN *walks back into the room—how did she get out there? Well, it should seem pretty magical, but it'll need to be a theatrical trick. A trapdoor or something. Anyhow,*

Neil LaBute

she walks back in, same as before, except this time holding the Tab can to her eye and carrying the magazine. She sets down the baby monitor and plops onto the couch.

MAN What I'm saying is, this is the way *she* described it to me, Belinda did, after it occurred. But, see, umm, I didn't really believe her . . . I mean, she *swears* it was this way, she does, but something seems a little off about it, and so that's why I made up the other story. The first one. Look, you decide for yourselves. (*Beat.*) Anyway, sorry about that. Told you before that you shouldn't totally trust me on any of this! . . .

The MAN *smiles and exits. After a moment, the* WOMAN *calls out.*

WOMAN . . . hello? (*Beat.*) I'm in here.
CODY (*offstage*) Why? Why're you in there?
WOMAN I just . . . because.

CODY *walks in, back from a run. Dressed the same as before but not nearly as sweaty. Wearing the sunglasses up on his head. He moves over toward his wife.*

CODY . . . hey. *Hey.* What happened?
WOMAN Oh, nothing, no, I just . . . I left the cupboard door open and . . .
CODY Baby, oww. Ouuw! Lemme see . . .

He crouches beside her, lifting the soda can to have a peek at his wife's condition.

CODY Damn . . .

WOMAN Bad?

CODY Mmm-hmm. Gonna be . . .

WOMAN Great. (*touches it*) Ouuuh . . .

CODY Hey, I'm the one who should be grumpy . . . the person who's gonna suffer is me. The shit I'll get for this'll be unbelievable . . .

WOMAN S'pose so. (*Beat.*) Good . . .

CODY People'll be saying I smacked you one. They totally will . . . (*Beat.*) "Black man goes on rampage," shit like that.

CODY *laughs at this, as does the* WOMAN. *She winces from the pain. He reaches over and kisses her gently.*

CODY There. Daddy'll make it all better.

WOMAN Mmmmm . . .

CODY You should probably use some ice, though. Honey? You should. Way more helpful than that soda pop . . .

WOMAN I know, but . . .

CODY You want me to get some?

WOMAN Yeah, but . . . in a minute. 'Kay?

CODY Sure.

CODY *pulls off his sweaty shirt and stretches—still looks good. He plops down on the couch near her, lifting up her legs and then pulling them onto his lap. She smiles.*

WOMAN Thanks . . . (*Beat.*) So, how're your protégés coming?

CODY Hmmm? Oh, they're, you know . . . don't know if they'll make state, but . . . working hard.

WOMAN That's good.

CODY Yeah.

WOMAN Nice of you to . . . you know, help out.

CODY Least I can do. I mean, I dump a ton 'a cash into that program, new *uniforms* and shit . . . might as well make sure some of the runners get their shot at a scholarship or, you know. Right?

WOMAN Sure. That's . . . Sure.

CODY Absolutely. (*Beat.*) Baby's okay?

WOMAN Yeah, he's sleeping . . .

CODY Good. That's cool. I know he's not feeling well, so . . .

WOMAN What time do you have to go in?

CODY Got a meeting at ten. Should be there a bit before . . .

WOMAN Why?

CODY You know, check in with everybody, do my e-mails and shit.

WOMAN Oh. Okay.

CODY . . . what? *What?*

WOMAN Nothing. I just . . . I was hoping you could take today off, it's Friday and, you know, it'd just be . . . we talked about you taking Fridays off once in a while.

CODY Yeah, but . . .

WOMAN No, I understand. We were gonna do the picnic thing with . . . but hey. (*Beat.*) Who're you meeting with?

CODY So tell 'em we'll get together and do something next week. 'S not a big deal. (*Beat.*) It's some people in from Chicago. Those, uhh, you know . . . I told you.

WOMAN No . . .

CODY . . . yeah, I did. The one guy's from, I don't know the place—Arlington Heights or whatever—they have the plant out there we want to use for that new line . . .

WOMAN Oh.

This Is How It Goes   **45**

CODY . . . the Adirondack line we're gonna add. All the
   furniture. Remember? (*Beat.*) I told you.

WOMAN Did you?

CODY Yes.

WOMAN Huh. Well, I must've forgot . . .

CODY Yeah. You just forgot or something, 'cause I told you.

WOMAN 'Kay.

CODY *kisses her on her bare feet and stands, wiping his neck
with the rumpled shirt.*

CODY I'm gonna hop in the shower . . . get myself ready.
   (*Beat.*) Hey, tell our *tenant* to mow that side yard today,
   would ya? I think he missed it last time . . .

WOMAN All right. (*Beat.*) That's a new one . . .

CODY What's that?

WOMAN Showering before work.

CODY What do you mean?

WOMAN I mean that you don't usually do that. Shower. Not
   before work, anyway . . .

CODY Yeah, I do.

WOMAN Uh-uh. Not usually . . . I mean, not if you've just been
   out with the team. Timing them or whatever.

CODY, *exasperated, throws his shirt on the end of the couch.
Comes over and hovers, leaning in dangerously close to
her.*

CODY Look . . .

WOMAN I'm just saying . . . just saying it, that's all.

CODY Well, don't, okay? We do not need all this jealousy crap.
'Kay?

WOMAN Fine. That's fine, Cody, whatever.

CODY *leans down a little closer to her, letting her get a good sniff.*

CODY . . . there, how's that? (*holds her head*) No, no, go on,
take a whiff. Nice, huh?

WOMAN . . . all right . . .

CODY No, seriously, a little more. Okay? You smell that? I'm
nasty right now, got clients coming, so just do not get into
your Desdemona shit. Have people to meet, that's all . . .

WOMAN Go, then. Should be nice . . . have a great lunch. Make
a bundle.

CODY There is just no talking to you . . .

WOMAN Yeah, well, I sorta like the truth tossed in there every
now and then when I'm chatting with a person . . . I'm just
funny that way.

CODY Oh shit . . . I'm outta here.

WOMAN Yep. Go. Maybe we'll have the food without you . . .
(*Beat.*) . . . go on.

CODY *throws his hands in the air—there really is no talking to
her some days. This seems to be one of them.*

CODY Yeah, I will. So I can make us some more money. Mo-ney
that you have no problem spending . . .

WOMAN I just spend it to piss you off.

CODY Well, hey, it works!

WOMAN Good . . .

CODY Yep, great. You have a *super* day, ho-ney . . .

WOMAN I will. Thanks. And tell her hi for me . . . whoever she is. *This* time.

CODY You are, like, so nuts . . . I mean it. Just completely crazy.

WOMAN Well, be proud of yourself, 'cause you made me this way . . .

CODY No, uh-uh, that is bullshit . . . total shit, and I'm not taking the fall on this one. (*Beat.*) You were pretty fucking out there when I first knew you, all the way back at school, but I *dealt* with it, that's what I did.

WOMAN That's great . . .

CODY You take the hand you're dealt, 's what my old man always said, and so I did it. And you, sweetness, were just one of the cards God threw my way . . .

WOMAN I really don't know what the hell you just said, but I'm sure it means something to you . . .

CODY You know exactly what I'm saying . . .

WOMAN No, Cody, I don't. I really don't.

CODY *moves closer to the* WOMAN. *Towering over her. She tries to hold her own, but hey, let's be honest. This guy can be a bit unnerving.*

CODY I'm saying that, had I been mature enough in high school to see past your *bangs* and your cute little cheerleader skirt, shit like that . . . I probably wouldn't be standing here, having this stupid fucking talk with you. Because you would not be in my house . . .

WOMAN Yeah? Well, I am now . . . but *you* can go. Just tell me

Neil LaBute

when and I'll help you pack up, have you outta here in under
an hour.

CODY I am not going nowhere.

WOMAN Well, that's a double negative, but I get your point . . .

CODY I bet you do. I bet you do at that. And I get yours . . .

WOMAN . . . and so there we are. Same lousy place we usually
find ourselves at.

CODY Yep.

WOMAN Great. That's really great . . .

CODY *starts off but stops, catching himself. Simmering.*

CODY Yeah, super. (*Beat.*) Okay, fine, you wanna know the
truth? Huh? Who I'm seeing on the side, 's that it? My *work*,
that's who. She's my fucking mistress . . .

WOMAN . . . right . . .

CODY It's true. I like it, I'm good at it, and it makes me happy.
I *love* making more money than any other guy in this town,
'cause it just pisses 'em off. I dig that. Plus, work doesn't
complain, or rag on me about shit, or leave those fucking
tampons wrapped in toilet paper in the trash for the dog to
drag down to the living room . . . so, yeah, I love my work. I
LOVE it, and there is not a damn thing that you can do about
it . . .

CODY *flicks his shirt at the wall. Exhales loudly.*

CODY This sucks. You know that? This whole thing, what
we've got here . . . or ended up with. It really sucks. It's
shit . . .

WOMAN No. It's *marriage*.

CODY *is about to respond when a child begins to whimper on the baby monitor. The parents look at each other.*

WOMAN . . . so?
CODY Hey, you're always saying "We both work, I just work here." So, get to *work* . . .

CODY *makes a dismissive gesture with his hand. Does it again.*

CODY Don't forget to tell Shakespeare to cut the grass . . .

And with that, CODY *is gone. The* WOMAN *sits for a moment, taking all this in. A long moment. Then she starts to cry. Not a lot—that's hard on an actor, and we've got a ways to go—but a little. Just enough.*

WOMAN (*to herself*) . . . it was *Othello* who was jealous! Not the other way around. Asshole.

The lights fade on her and up slowly on the MAN, *who is now standing in his old spot. He's changed his clothes—not too much, but khakis and a shirt, tennis shoes—and seems ready to go somewhere.*

MAN . . . see what I mean? I don't really know the whole story, but those two have got something going on. Some sorta trouble. They do . . . (*Beat.*) I mean, it's a *detached* garage and all, but hey . . . voices carry.

Lights slowly rise on a new playing space while the MAN *is talking. A sort of backyard, with maybe a barbecue pit or that type of thing. A picnic table. We won't use it just yet, but I wanted to give you a heads-up.*

MAN . . . we're gonna be together again in a minute—the three of us, I mean—so I just wanted to grab a second here and sort of set this up, let you know what's going on. By the way, funny how you never see the kids, isn't it? It's not weird or anything, like in *Virginia Woolf* or whatever . . . it's just a personal choice. We thought that might be too much, plus kids're hard as shit to work with—not them themselves, I mean, I like kids, I do—but the labor laws and tutors and all that crap, so we just decided against 'em. Or plan to, after this gets finished and somebody decides to stage the thing . . . anyhow, what I'm saying is: Children are great, but you ain't gonna see any of 'em tonight! Okay? Good.

CODY *and the* WOMAN *enter now, each taking up positions in the backyard space.* CODY *is manning the grill, and she is busy setting the table. Plates, forks, napkins. That sort of deal. The* MAN *looks over at them and smiles.*

MAN . . . they really are a pretty great-looking couple. I mean, when you just see them together, from afar. Problem is, I think it has to be *really* afar, because otherwise you might hear what they're saying to each other! Still, they are very attractive people . . . and in a way, that makes all this somewhat, umm, sadder. Not that I . . . well, watch what happens. You'll see what I mean. Sorry! I'm being so *cryptic,* and I don't mean to be. Just watch. It's all gonna be okay in the end. It will, I promise . . .

He smiles out at us and then moves off, toward CODY *and the* WOMAN. *They spot him coming—*CODY *turns back to his grill, and the* WOMAN *stands to greet the* MAN. *They hug;* CODY *catches it.*

MAN . . . hello!

WOMAN Oh! Hi there . . .

MAN Hey. (*looking around*) Where're the kids?

WOMAN Oh, you know, around. Cody Jr.'s at a play date. Baby's asleep.

MAN Great. That's nice . . . (*another hug*) Hi.

CODY Shit. (*Beat.*) Don't mind me . . .

They laugh at this—not CODY, *of course, but the* MAN *and the* WOMAN. *They break their hug, and she goes back to setting up drink cups. The* MAN *tries to help out.*

MAN Sorry. It's just . . .

CODY What?

MAN I dunno. Great to see you guys . . . I mean, *both* of you.

CODY Yeah? Well, then, you better get over here and gimme a big cuddle, too, while you're at it. I don't wanna be left outta the *lovefest.*

The MAN *chuckles, then decides to call* CODY*'s bluff. He moves toward the grill, but* CODY *holds up his chef tools in a makeshift cross.*

MAN . . . I luv you, man.

CODY Get the fuck outta here!

The men pretend to hug, then back away from each other. The WOMAN *smiles at this as she starts on the plastic cutlery.*

CODY . . . and you didn't bring your cards, I see.

MAN Oh, damn! Sorry. You want me to run back over and . . . ?

CODY Nah, we can do it later. What took you so long? (*checks his watch*) It's already ten after . . .

MAN Oh, yeah, sorry . . . I was finishing up this movie. On TV. Had to let it wrap up . . . that's the best part.

CODY What, the end? .

MAN Uh-huh.

WOMAN Why, to see what happens?

MAN Well, sure, yeah . . . but to see who ends up with whom. How they all get paired off. The characters, I mean . . .

WOMAN Oh. Right . . .

CODY . . . *okay* . . .

MAN No, seriously . . . I love that. Trying to guess who'll end up together. Or if. *If* they will. As a writer, I find it really interesting . . .

CODY Cool. (*Beat.*) You want steak or some chicken? I got burgers, too.

MAN Ummm . . . maybe a little of each. That all right?

CODY Yep. Same thing I'm doing. High on the protein. No carbs . . .

MAN Great.

CODY *turns to a covered plate and begins taking off the foil to get at the meat. The* MAN *decides to return and help the* WOMAN. *He picks up a pitcher and starts pouring drinks.*

WOMAN . . . so, what was on? The TV, I mean.

MAN Oh, it was this Hitchcock thing . . .

WOMAN Nice. Which one?

MAN No, it was a, like, some tribute or something. On cable . . .

WOMAN Oh.

MAN All weekend. They're playing a *ton* of his films . . . one right after the other. It's pretty great.

WOMAN I like Hitchcock . . . I think Cody does, too. Don't you, honey?

CODY What's that?

WOMAN Like Hitchcock movies . . .

CODY Not much. They're all right. *The Birds* was good . . . (*Beat.*) Anyways, I thought you were some *playwright*, so why the hell you spend all day in front of the movies?

WOMAN . . . anyway . . . (*to the* MAN) Let's—

MAN You liked *The Birds*, huh, Cody? That sounds suspiciously like you having *fun* . . .

CODY Yeah, time 'a my life . . .

CODY *slaps some meat on the grill, seasons it, and puts down the lid. Opens the little steam valve.*

WOMAN And what were you watching? I mean, before you came over . . .

MAN Oh, right. Yeah, I was finishing up *Strangers on a Train*. Tonight is *Vertigo*, and this morning was that one with, ummm . . . *Shadow of a Doubt*. Plus, there's one of the lesser ones later, at midnight.

WOMAN Really? Which one . . . I like him, maybe I'll watch it.

CODY You already said that. Said you liked Hitchcock already . . .

WOMAN I know, I was just—

CODY . . . just so you do. Know.

MAN It's, umm, *Marnie*. I think.

WOMAN Oh. Good.

CODY The one about the liar . . . (*Beat.*) I'm gonna go get the veggies.

WOMAN . . . check on the baby, would ya?

CODY *nods and heads off toward the kitchen—any of the exits will do. We just need to get him offstage. The* MAN *stops him.*

MAN . . . you mean "thief."

CODY What?

MAN She's a thief, in the film. *Marnie*. Or, Tippi Hedren is, the actress. She's a thief in that one . . .

CODY Oh, I thought she was both. Anyway, same difference . . . *philosophically* speaking.

MAN Really? How's that?

CODY She steals shit, right?

MAN Yeah . . .

CODY Well, liars just steal the truth . . . 'S the same thing. It's all theft.

And with that, CODY *exits. The* MAN *and* WOMAN *are left looking at each other—that's okay, they don't mind. An easy smile between them.*

MAN . . . man's got a point.

WOMAN He always does—he is happy to tell you. (*whispers*) And it usually has to do with his *mother* . . .

MAN Ahhh, right. (*Beat.*) Well, too bad they didn't offer a "philosophy" course at school . . . he might've aced it.

WOMAN Probably. He does always get what he wants . . .

MAN Yeah?

WOMAN Oh, yeah. *Always.*

MAN Even you? I mean . . .

The WOMAN *looks hard at the* MAN, *unsure how to respond. She looks back at the house, then moves over toward him.*

WOMAN . . . no. He got me because I wanted him to. That's how.

MAN Really?

WOMAN Yes. From that first time I saw Cody . . . on the bus. The activity bus home one night. Right from then.

MAN . . . wow.

WOMAN Uh-huh.

MAN That's so . . . great. Really.

WOMAN Why? Why is that great?

MAN Oh, you know, because . . . it's true love and all that. Right?

WOMAN . . . you sure it's not just because I like a nice, thick black cock? Hmm? Maybe that's why . . .

She tries to smile but has to look away, blushing. The MAN *stops for a moment, as if stunned by this. He then moves down center. Toward us.*

MAN . . . okay, obviously she didn't say it like that. I mean, it's *obvious*, right? She's not that way, would never say a thing like that . . . God, can you picture *her* saying that?! *Anything* like that? (*laughs*) No way, not at all. Or any girl, really. Not any that I know. Maybe, like, in a *movie* or something, but real people? Uh-uh. *But*, see . . . it is what *I'm* thinking right now. Or then. I mean, what I've had in my head since the first time I heard about her and Cody. Or anytime you see a white girl and a . . . well, you know. And it is a cliché, I'm aware of that, but it's hard not to . . . I mean, most everybody knows those jokes, or stories, or whatever you wanna call 'em. And so I can't help it if that's what I'm imagining right now . . . I can't! And anyhow, a cliché is just a thing that's true, usually. Some true thing that gets said over and over . . . (*Beat.*) But no, she never said that. Or will. Or will *ever*. Not her. Not Belinda Rivers. That was her maiden name . . . Rivers. I bet she's never said that before. "Cock." Not even lying in bed, with him, or . . . Jesus, he may be the only guy she's ever laid in bed with! I mean, it's possible. Shit, that's . . . whoah. Could you imagine? Damn. (*Beat.*) Anyway, we need to be careful here, be as true to this as we can, so, no . . . she'd never say that. About Cody's, you know . . . *thing*. That was all me. Not that *I* was thinking about his—you know—just that . . . o-kay, let's drop it . . .

The MAN *shrugs and returns to the picnic table, back there next to the* WOMAN, *who is turned and lost in thought. Just like we left her. Well, that's convenient.*

MAN That's so . . . great. Really.
WOMAN Why? Why is that great?
MAN Oh, you know, because . . . it's true love and all that. Right?

WOMAN . . . people don't really use those words anymore, do
they? I mean, not in a long time . . .

MAN No. I s'pose not. But it's a nice thought all the same . . .

The WOMAN *stands and goes to check the grill. She lifts the lid
and turns the pieces of meat one by one. The* MAN *rises to
stand near her.*

WOMAN . . . I wanted to be noticed. That's what it was.

MAN Hmmm?

WOMAN The reason I first . . . oh, nothing.

MAN No, go ahead. Please.

WOMAN When I said yes to Cody, the time he asked me out—
bowling or to the skating rink, I don't remember now—I said
okay because I thought it would make me stand out.

MAN Really?

WOMAN Sure. That's the problem with high school—one of the
many problems, anyway. You're so desperate to fit in, and at
the same time totally needing to stand out . . .

MAN Exactly. Yeah, I mean . . . yes.

WOMAN You know? And for me, well . . . I guess I never really
stopped. Doing this, I mean, marrying Cody and staying
here—if you could've seen my dad's face!—it's sad, really.
Not sad, I suppose, but . . . pathetic, almost. That I need
people to be aware of me that badly. Doesn't matter what
you look like or how smart you are. No. It's really how you
feel about yourself. Who you are. And I was raised with the
total sense that I wasn't good enough . . . or that I wouldn't
make the right choices. That's it. My parents were always
nervous that I'd make some mistake along the way, even in
preschool! And so, at some point . . . that is what I decided

Neil LaBute

to do. Prove 'em right. I made a "mistake" they'd never forget. (*Beat.*) But I was in love, too. I shouldn't sound— well, actually I *shouldn't* be saying any of this, but—I loved him. Cody. When we got married. I really think I did . . . but, then, it didn't hurt that he was rich and black and different. Especially the last one. Rich, I don't care so much about. I mean, it's okay . . . and black, well, that wasn't such a bad thing, either. But different? Now, that's a good one . . . I like *different*. Or at least thought I did . . .

The WOMAN *looks at the* MAN, *to gauge his reaction. He nods and looks back toward the house. They both do—hey, they're not stupid.*

MAN . . . oh.

WOMAN Yeah. "Oh." As in, oh-oh . . .

MAN That's funny. I mean, *interesting*.

WOMAN Not really.

MAN But it's . . . is that true?

WOMAN Yes. Mostly. Because doing that, marrying him, it made me different, too. And I still get some kind of thrill from it . . . walking into an Arby's or through Wal-Mart with these two brown children in tow. My little *pickaninnies*—that's what my parents call them—with their light-colored eyes. I do. I mean, it might be old hat in a place like New York or wherever, but around here . . . it's still a pretty big deal. (*Beat.*) These faces turning 'round to get a look at us, the whispering, and me with this fat checkbook and my head all held up. Defiant. I don't even know why I like it so much. I just do . . .

MAN Wow.

WOMAN Yeah. "Wow." Scary . . .

MAN No, it's . . . why? Why "scary"?

WOMAN . . . scary that I'm that needy.

She looks at the MAN, *and he trails off. Tries to smile.*

MAN No, not at all . . . (*Beat.*) Listen, this is going to sound
lame, so I'm preparing you now, but . . . see, I always
thought you stood out. Completely. I mean, *so* much . . .

WOMAN Huh. Well . . .

MAN Wow, that was even worse than I thought! I mean,
seriously sad. Forgive me.

WOMAN No way. I'm keeping that . . . it's all mine.

MAN What?

WOMAN Just that, you know, little tidbit. You put it out there,
so I get to have it . . . and thank you.

MAN "Pleasure"—he says, glancing around to see if the
husband is about to plunge a steak knife into his back . . .

They both laugh at this—good, that's nice. Just like before.

WOMAN . . . I think you're in the clear. For a minute, anyway.

MAN That's all I need. A minute. I'm much faster than I used to
be . . .

WOMAN Yeah, but he'll kill ya out in the open. It's in the flats,
that's the problem . . .

MAN Damn that Flyin' Cody Phipps!

They laugh again—but they'd better be careful. CODY *'s coming.
At the last moment, they both notice.*

WOMAN Hey, sweetie!

MAN Cody . . . you need any help?

CODY Nah, I'm good . . . (*Beat.*) Wouldn't wanna break up your *coffee klatch* there.

WOMAN We were just . . .

MAN . . . talking, you know . . .

CODY Yeah, yeah, I know. I do know. Was watching you from the window there, in the kitchen, and . . . boy, you two are like a couple old nannies!

MAN That's us!

WOMAN I was checking the meat for you, and we just got to . . .

CODY Funny, he never talks that much when I'm around. Does he?

MAN (*looking around*) Are you . . . I mean, do you mean *me*? 'Cause I'm standing right here.

CODY I know *exactly* where you are. Believe me . . .

WOMAN Honey, please don't . . .

CODY Doesn't bother me. Not at all. You can knock yourselves out . . . I just noticed it. That's all.

CODY *takes a quick peek at the grill and then, satisfied, finds himself a nearby chair. He looks at the two of them.*

CODY . . . carry on.

WOMAN I think most of this is ready. Umm, maybe not the cutlets . . .

MAN . . . yeah, I think chicken's supposed to be—

CODY Give it a minute. (*Beat.*) So, what's up? What're you guys blabbing your heads off about? Hmm?

WOMAN Oh, just, you know . . .

CODY Nope. I don't. I do not.

MAN Just, stuff, really. Life stuff . . .

CODY What's that mean?

MAN I dunno. We were *chatting*, that's all.

CODY But not about you, I'll bet. (*Beat.*) Am I right?

MAN What's that mean?

WOMAN Cody, honey, let's just . . . would you check these burgers, please?

CODY I said leave it. Shit. They're fine. (*to the* MAN) I'm saying I could see you both yakking on out here about shit, but my guess is . . . you didn't say a damn thing about yourself.

MAN Why do you say that?

CODY 'Cause I've noticed it. Times we've been together . . . like pulling *molars* outta your skull to get anything at all personal . . .

The MAN *backs away a little—I never really noticed it, but maybe* CODY*'s right about him. The* MAN *sits at the table.*

MAN . . . that's true. I'm not the most open guy around. Yeah.

CODY Well, that's big of you . . .

MAN Cody, look . . .

WOMAN . . . sweetie . . .

CODY No, seriously. I know ya know about us, ya leave your damn *windows* open all day and night—but I don't got hardly two bits of info on you. Was a lawyer. Has a kid. That's it . . .

WOMAN I'm turning the grill off . . .

The WOMAN *does so. She starts moving the meat from the*
metal rack inside the grill to a large serving plate. The MAN
takes a drink, then smiles at CODY.

MAN . . . because those're the highlights. Honestly, not much
    to tell.

CODY Bullshit. Everybody's got a story. *Every*-body . . .

MAN 'S that right? What's mine, then? I mean, if you're so sure
    and all . . .

WOMAN Guys, can we just . . . ?

MAN No, it's okay. It's fine. He's got something he wants to
    say, so we should probably just hear it . . .

CODY Yeah?

MAN Go for it.

CODY 'Kay . . . Well, let's see. You told us about your daughter.
    Not much, but some. *Enough.* Enough to know that's not the
    sore spot . . .

MAN Did I forget to trim your hedges or something? I mean,
    Cody, what is up with this . . . ?

CODY Nothing. Just playing with you . . .

MAN No, you're not. Uh-uh. You've got a thought, so let's hear
    it. *What?*

CODY . . . all right. Fine. (*Beat.*) Why're you really back here?
    And none of your smart-mouth answers . . . why did you stop
    being a lawyer? That's not something people really do. Give
    up a good job like that. Not usually.

The MAN *looks long and hard at* CODY, *then over at the* WOMAN.
She's making herself a burger, but she's listening. No doubt
about that.

This Is How It Goes   63

MAN . . . I just did, that's all. Okay? Just up and quit one day, had my fill of it and walked out. Cleared out my things, and I was . . . done.

CODY Huh . . . pretty generic. (*Beat.*) Plus, a theater writer and living out *here*? I don't think so.

MAN Writers can live anywhere, Cody. That's kind of the *point* . . .

Both CODY *and the* WOMAN *watch the* MAN, *realizing that he doesn't wish to go any further. In a way, though, he needs to. This is the right moment.*

WOMAN . . . don't feel like you have to . . .

CODY Don't do that. All right? Don't just always jump in to defend every damn person I have a conversation with. It is pretty fucking annoying . . . (*Beat.*) The guy can just tell me to shut up, if he wants . . .

WOMAN I know that. I *know*. I only wanted to make this nice, have some food out on the lawn. I'm sorry . . .

The marrieds stare each other down—to her credit, the WOMAN *is holding her own.*

MAN . . . no, Cody's right. That's a total crock—company-line shit. I had to sign a statement, actually, that I would tell that story, or something like it, as what happened, so I got used to it, I guess. Yep. (*Beat.*) But you guys, well . . . you're friends of mine, right? I can tell you the truth. Sure. (*to the* WOMAN) Do you mind if I have one of the burgers?

The WOMAN *nods, starts fixing him one. The* MAN *watches her as he talks; the* WOMAN *brings one each to the* MAN *and to* CODY.

Neil LaBute

MAN . . . I was let go. "Fired," I guess, is the term they used to use when our fathers were alive. Well, maybe not your father, Cody, because he was a self-made guy, but my old man was a mechanic, worked at that Union 76 over on McHenry all his life, and if he screwed up—like, totally ruined somebody's car or mouthed off to the owner—then he would get fired. He wasn't, no . . . but I was. Me. I was fired. For something I did.

WOMAN . . . I think I'm going to go inside.

MAN No, please don't. Okay? I want you to hear this, Belinda. Need you to. Because I haven't really told anyone, so it feels good. Not *good*, but you know . . . freeing, somehow.

WOMAN Are you sure you . . . ?

CODY Just let the man talk.

MAN Thanks. Yeah. Well, does everybody have what they want, for lunch, I mean? Because after this, we may not be . . . just checking. (*Beat.*) I was a good lawyer, fair, anyway. I was very fair with people, and decent. And that's not an easy thing, in that job. Not at all, but I was. Anyhow, I'm on a business trip one time, with some of the people from my office, we were going to, ummm, Pittsburgh or someplace, I don't remember, but we're late for the plane—it was on United, I recall that, it was with United. And I got there a little late, maybe twenty minutes before the flight closed, but a friend, this dude I knew from law school, is up there getting his boarding pass, and he lets me slip in. Into line. Ahead of a few other colleagues . . . and one of them, this lady named Carol, an African-American woman who worked with us, says something out loud. Not a big deal, like, "Hey, no cuts," or something, but you know, the kind of day it was, all rainy and a race through the terminal, I just wasn't in the mood. Not at all. *Yet* I let it go. I do. I get my thingie and even use some miles to get bumped up—the last guy to be able to do it, they are totally sold out—and off we go, my buddy and me, down toward security and to the gate. I make eye contact with ol' Carol on the way, toss her a smile, and we're off. Actually, we stop by Mickey D's and grab a McRib each. Those're really good . . .

The MAN *takes a breather;* CODY *and the* WOMAN *are still there, hanging on his words.* CODY *heard the "African-American" thing, and his antennae are up.*

CODY . . . where's this going?
WOMAN Honey, he's trying to—
CODY I'm just asking.
MAN I'm sorry, I'm rambling. Lemme just get to the . . . we get on the plane. So, we're sitting there in first, having our pre-takeoff ginger ale or whatever, and people are filing past, bashing into me—I'm on the aisle—with their two bags each, and we're talking away, and bam!, I get tagged again by some computer case. Right on the elbow. And it hurts, it really does, so I'm about to say something . . . when I glance up, it's Carol. Not even looking. Heading back into economy—thanks to me, in all probability—and it just makes my associate and me start laughing. I mean *howling*, really, the two of us, there in the cabin.
   At some point, I'm not sure when, a bit later—I thought a *lot* later, but—I lean over to him, I lean in a bit and say, really whispering, "Well, at least they still sit in the back of the bus." Just for fun, right? It's this little joke, we're on an *Airbus*, after all, and I swear to God, the place goes silent.

Neil LaBute

Like a church for a moment, when the A/C is about to switch over or something . . . I say this thing and a bunch of folks are suddenly looking right down at me. Including *Carol*. See, some old lady back there is messing around with her suitcase, this old Samsonite, and the line hasn't moved. Carol is, I mean, she is standing *right* there. Shit . . . I start to sputter, try to stand up, my belt is hooked, and it jerks me back into my seat, I spill the drink. A whole parade. I do finally get to my feet and try to explain, say, "What I meant to say was . . ." and she tears into me, well, it was pretty unbelievable. 'S like *Angela Davis* has suddenly appeared, and she's all waving her hands and screaming at me—you know how black women can get—with the "motherfuckin' " this and that, like she'd never been to school a day in her life! And I . . . I lost it. I admit it, I just totally lost it there for a bit . . . and I grabbed her by both her shoulders, this Carol woman, not hard or anything, but grabbed her and shook her a second. I shook her and said, "Hey, Carol, stop it! Stop acting like some *blue-gummed chimp*, just fell outta the tree!" (*Beat.*) So . . . just imagine what the next five minutes were like, those last few moments when I'm standing and collecting my stuff . . . it was just so unreal. No, *sur*real. I will never forget that feeling . . . And I didn't apologize, that's the thing. Which is what really does me in, I guess. See, they wanted this formal letter of . . . anyway, I just wouldn't do it. I wasn't gonna back down. I was *defiant*. The firm "let me go" about three days later. Well, I guess suspended first, but then . . . yeah. My wife left a few weeks after that. Not because it bothered her, I don't think, but because it was the *right* thing to do. Or gave her an excuse, anyway. This was almost a year ago. And *that* is who you are renting your apartment to. (*Beat.*) Anyway, Cody, how's that burger?

CODY *takes another bite before he says anything. Maybe two.*

WOMAN Maybe we should . . . I don't know. What should we do now? Cody?

CODY *wipes his mouth with one hand, then finds his napkin. Uses it. Stands.*

CODY Me? I'm gonna go check out the dish . . . maybe that *Hitchcock* movie you're both so excited about.
MAN You did ask . . .
CODY Yeah, I know. Don't mean you always gotta tell the truth.
WOMAN Cody, we still have all this . . .
CODY Then wrap it up. Save it for the kids, I don't give a damn . . .
MAN Maybe I'll head back over to—
CODY No, you guys have a nice chat. Go on. Like nothing happened. And it didn't, right? Nothing happened. Other than we found out what a piece of shit we got living here with us . . .

The MAN *starts to say something, then stops. The* WOMAN *moves to* CODY, *but he shakes her off. Holds up a finger.*

CODY (toward the MAN) . . . you need to get gone. Outta this place. Right? End of the month.

CODY *wanders off toward the house. Exits. The* MAN *and the* WOMAN *sit quietly for a moment. Maybe even longer—no hugs*

Neil LaBute

this time. Just silence. Then, out of nowhere, her hand touches the MAN*'s hand. She holds it. Now, this is interesting.*

WOMAN . . . well. I'm sure he's—I mean, he usually doesn't stay mad long . . .

MAN Doesn't matter.

WOMAN No?

MAN Uh-uh. Glad I said it. Needed to.

WOMAN Then good. People should do what they need to do. Mostly.

MAN Yeah. (*stands*) I'm gonna go back upstairs, is that okay?

WOMAN Oh, please. Sure. Yes. I'll just . . . I'm gonna clean some of this up.

MAN Do you want any . . . ?

WOMAN No, I'm fine. Absolutely.

MAN 'Kay. Sorry.

WOMAN No, don't be, it's . . . it was only *lunch*, right?

MAN Right. I'll see you, then.

WOMAN You, too.

MAN: Later.

He moves off, down toward us. She remains and clears the table.

MAN: . . . so, that was different, huh? Very. Hey, maybe that'll make her like me more or something. She says she likes *different*. And I am that, if nothing else . . . (*Beat.*) Speaking of Belinda, and I should've done this earlier, but . . . hey. One thing you should know—or should've known—about us. We did kiss once. Yes. I don't mean in the past, not at the *drive-in* or anything, but recently. Like, within the last few weeks.

Not a big deal, I mean, it was very nice, don't get me wrong
. . . but it was just this small little thing. It was. Or will be.
Out on the lawn here one time, when I'm cutting the side
yard. I was—or will be—ahh, mowing, like I said, or I guess
. . . maybe I was raking at that point. Yeah, raking, and . . .
(*Beat.*) . . . we kiss. That's pretty much it. Just this nice
kiss that comes from her bringing me a glass of tap water,
something to cool me off. Didn't work! Not after . . . not
after doing that. With her. I wasn't or will not be—I am not
cool after that! And it's out of nowhere, that's the thing that
really knocks me out . . . we just kiss. We kiss like there's a
respirator between us and our lips are the only thing keeping
the other person going. You know how that is, when you're
with someone and you get a bit close, sort of begin to cross
the *demilitarized zone* and there's no going back . . . that's
how it went. Amazing.

The MAN *drifts for a moment, remembering it. Let's give him
some space—it sounds like it was kind of great. We probably
should've shown it before, but too late now. Or is it?*

MAN But hey . . . if you guys wanna see, we can probably show
you. The kiss, at least. The thing itself. It's a bit weird, to do
it over again, I mean, you know, after all the other stuff that
you've . . . but we can pull it off. No problem. Here.

*He takes off his shirt, pitches it out of the way. Finds a weed-
eater somewhere onstage—that's the designer's problem. The*
MAN *starts working on the feeder (where the fishing line comes
out of the thing), and suddenly, the* WOMAN *appears. Glass of
water in her hand. Ice cubes. The* MAN *looks up.*

*She smiles at him, holding up the drink. He takes the tumbler
and gulps down the cool liquid. She smiles and, without
thinking, reaches over and wipes his brow. He smiles back. And
then they're kissing—kind of surprising, but believe me, it's
happening. This goes on for a few moments. When they stop,
she leans over and steals a sip from the glass. Moves off.*

The MAN *watches her go. Wistful. Unsure. He shakes it off and
looks back at us. Starts changing his clothing—he's going to
need some jogging stuff. Sweats. Shoes. Nothing too fancy.*

MAN . . . see, I told you—it was pretty nice. I don't know if you
could tell that from where you guys're sitting, but . . . it was
really so damn nice. (*Beat.*) There's a name for that area
there, way up in the last rows . . . you know what it is? It's
slang, but it's funny as hell! Check it out sometime, it's in
that *Oxford* dictionary. I'll give you a clue. It's under "N."

The MAN *stretches now, shaking out his limbs. Trying to loosen
up a bit.*

MAN . . . you know, while we're gettin' so fancy—like, back in
time and all that—we should probably take a look at
something that happened a while ago. I mean, not as long
ago as the kiss, not that far back, but before now. Or before
now later, when this part happens. Right? Anyway, it's worth
checking out, 'cause it definitely puts a wrinkle in things.
Yeah, adds a little . . . Well, you'll see.

CODY *enters, wearing running gear again and sweating through
it. Sits down and starts stretching out.*

MAN Cody and I met up once . . . over at this nature preserve where they have these running trails. A mile or so from here. A few weeks after the whole lawn-party thing. We hooked up and went for a jog. This is how it goes . . .

The MAN *wanders over near* CODY *and drops down, starts his own form of stretching. Gradually,* CODY *glances at him.*

MAN . . . hello. Hey.

CODY What's up?

MAN Not much.

CODY All right. Here . . .

CODY *stands up and unzips a large pocket on the front of his windbreaker. Pulls out a business envelope and hands it over to the* MAN. *The* MAN *opens it, counting out a stack of bills.*

CODY . . . 's your deposit.

MAN Uh-huh. (*stops*) Kind of *niggardly*, isn't it?

CODY Would you can it with that shit? It is not funny . . .

MAN I'm joking! It's a *joke* . . . (*Beat.*) You know what the word means, don't ya?

CODY Yeah, I do. I understand, but that don't make it cool.

MAN Okay, sorry. (*taps his leg*) You're not gonna take anything out for my changing the *carpet*?

CODY Ha-ha. Real cute . . .

MAN Just asking.

CODY *shakes his head; the* MAN *smiles and jams the thick wad of money into his warm-up pants. He reaches into another pocket and produces a single baseball card inside a thick plastic case. Hands it to* CODY, *who marvels at it and pops it into his front pocket. Zips it closed.*

CODY Thanks . . . (*Beat.*) I don't like this. I don't like meeting up out here . . . wanna be careful.

MAN Fine. That's all right. I just needed some cash . . .

CODY Whatever.

MAN Had to rent a new place, buy a few *knickknacks*, that sort of thing . . . moving's not easy.

CODY Good. Well, now you've got a little spending money.

MAN Thank you. Thanks, Cody.

CODY Yeah, yeah. Right.

MAN That means a lot to me . . .

CODY Just shut up, okay? Really . . . don't. (*Beat.*) So, are we good?

MAN Yep.

CODY Fine. (*Beat.*) . . . How many times've you seen her now? I mean, since then. That day.

MAN A few. Six, maybe . . .

CODY Six? She's called you *six* times?

MAN Something like that . . . and yes, I make sure she calls from the *house.* Leaving a paper trail . . .

CODY Fine. Okay. And you've met . . . ?

MAN . . . a couple.

CODY I don't want to know any more than that.

MAN Great.

CODY *shakes out his limbs, getting ready to run.*

CODY . . . but you guys aren't . . . I mean, you haven't, umm . . . right? Not yet.

MAN That's really . . . not your business. Isn't that what we
discussed? That was up to my discretion . . .

CODY No, yeah, true, I was just . . .

MAN . . . believe me, it's better not to. *I'm* the one used to be
the lawyer, remember?

CODY 'Course I do. It's the only reason the two of us are even
standing here. (*Beat*.) How much longer, you figure?

MAN What, until you can say something? Or catch us? Hell, I
dunno . . . give it a month or so. Don't ya think?

CODY Yeah. That's . . . I s'pose.

MAN You seem anxious . . .

CODY Of course I am. Come on!

MAN Of course you are . . . (*Beat*.) Who is she, by the way?

CODY What?

MAN The girl I saw you with . . . out by the reservoir. Last
week. She's cute, but really young.

CODY No, that's the . . . I'm training her. She's on the track
team at—

MAN *Right*. Look, I know you've told the wife that you're in love
with your work, I know that—she told me as much—but
please, Cody, do me the favor. I'm a *guy*. I can smell *chick*
on you a mile away . . .

CODY No, seriously, I'm not . . . no.

MAN Hey, whatever it takes to sleep at night. Knock yourself out.

CODY I don't know what you're saying . . .

MAN I'm saying, pretty outright, that a person does not do this,
this *Mayor of Casterbridge* thing you've got going here,
without some reason. A reason like the one I saw you out
running with.

CODY No, shit, that is . . . it's not anything. I just wanted to get
this Jackie Robinson card back, so I . . .

MAN Cody, please. Be honest here. You did not ask me to go in with you on this racket, our little shell game we're running, just so you could put some piece 'a *cardboard* back into your collection . . . (*Beat.*) You asked me to take your wife— have her in *trade*—if I'd help you pull it off. For shit like that, I mean, *that* elaborate . . . there is always a reason.

CODY No, we just got to talking . . . I mean, at the airport . . . we got to talking about that card and then, I dunno, we . . .

MAN Cody, I was *there*, remember? Right there next to you. You asked me this flat out. Told me your story. The "disgruntled hubby, the trophy wife," the whole damn business.

CODY Yeah, but I knew you liked her . . . back in school, I'm saying. I came to you because I was . . . because . . .

MAN No, I *came* up to you . . . saw you and made the connection, came over and, like, *three* beers later . . . you dish up this proposition. A *whopper* of a proposition . . .

CODY I'd just been thinking, that's all! Thinkin' about it. (*Beat.*) You did always like her. I know that . . .

MAN So, you were just being nice, then? Gonna let me have her as a *gift*?

CODY No, I . . .

MAN You gave me your wife. *Asked* me to take her. Now, you're either *Henny Youngman*, or there's something fishy going on! (*Beat.*) I'm only saying this to help remind you—do not forget the truth here. The truth is always of some importance.

CODY *stares at the* MAN, *not sure how he knows all this. Suddenly, the* MAN *seems a lot sharper than he's come off during the rest of the proceedings.*

CODY . . . you must've been a damn smart lawyer.

MAN I was okay. Just all right. I didn't have the stomach for it. So?

CODY So, yeah . . . yes. Her. She's . . . I do not need people knowing about that. She's in school, and I don't—

MAN Good. I just want to know the how and why of it. Nothing more.

CODY Fine. That's fine. That is a long-term project. My *own* business.

MAN Yes, it is. Keep it that way, okay? You've hidden it this long, do not screw it up now . . . (*looking around*) I don't like standing here, just yakking away like this. Maybe we should jog . . .

CODY What . . . you and me?

MAN Yeah. Makes it look all natural. Just like two "buddies" out for a run. Keepin' in shape.

CODY I'd kill you in a race . . .

MAN I didn't say "race." I said "jog." You've got *race* on the brain, my man . . .

CODY You just don't stop, do ya?

MAN Hey . . . by any means necessary. Isn't that what you people always say?

CODY Stop! Come on, dude, knock it off.

MAN Okay . . .

The two men begin to "jog"—basically running in place, but we'll work that out as we go. They move in silence for a bit, then start to talk again.

CODY By the way . . . that shit about the woman on the plane was not funny. At all.

Neil LaBute

MAN Hah! Sorry 'bout that . . . spur-of-the-moment thing.

CODY Yeah, well . . .

MAN It worked, didn't it?

CODY Yes, it worked. Worked at pissing me off, that's what it did . . .

MAN Listen, we could've gone on like that, me living upstairs and typing away, sneaking glances at the Mrs. for the next *eight* months. I made a move, did a little jump-start, that was all . . .

CODY You didn't have to go there . . . say bullshit like that.

MAN Cody, it was a perfect step, okay? Per-fect. While you were in getting the kabobs, Belinda told me a story out there, something about her that made me feel that I should make a play like that . . . and it worked.

CODY I hate that kinda thing, just so you know. Any kind of racist shit. Just so you're aware . . .

MAN I know. Of course I know. That's *why* I did it . . .

CODY I need her out of my home, but I don't wanna go through all this crap to do it. Otherwise, fuck, I might as well just get a *divorce* . . .

MAN Hey, you *are* going to get divorced! You'll have to . . . you're just going to get everything that you want *in* the divorce. That's why I'm here.

CODY . . . right . . .

MAN Isn't that what we agreed to?

CODY Yeah. It is.

MAN All right, then. So don't let a tiny bit of prejudice get in the way of what we're doing . . . (*Beat.*) That thing on the plane happened. I just never lost my job over it. I said it, had a good laugh with my co-worker, and enjoyed a first-class dinner all the way to Pittsburgh. I'm not a lawyer anymore

This Is How It Goes

because I decided to get back into writing, that's all. I am not married now because it didn't work out—I was a liar and a mediocre husband—but I'm gonna try harder next time. *And* I don't see my kid that often because she's a girl and, frankly, I'm just not that into it. (*Beat.*) That's all there really is to my story . . .

CODY Oh.

MAN Yep. "Oh." As in oh-oh . . .

CODY What?

MAN Nothing. Just something I heard . . .

The men stop running for a moment. Make that, the MAN *stops (holding his side), and* CODY *holds up for him.*

CODY Tired?

MAN Yeah, hold on a sec, lemme catch my breath.

CODY You gotta push through the pain . . .

MAN . . . you gotta back off for a minute, let me worry about my own self.

CODY Once a fatty, always a fatty. Ya probably got a weak heart. Kidneys.

The MAN *takes in a few deep breaths, trying to fight off a cramp. Flips* CODY *the finger.* CODY *wanders about, keeping warm and stretching.*

MAN . . . hey, we can't all be Olympians. Or *almost* Olympians.

CODY Whatever.

MAN I mean, you did nearly make it, right? That's what I heard.

CODY Something like that . . .

MAN Not that I used to search all over the Internet for news of the past or whatnot, but . . . you know.

CODY Yeah.

MAN Word gets around.

CODY Great.

MAN So what happened? You were good.

CODY Uh-huh. Well, "good" don't mean shit. Not out there. Not in sports.

MAN True.

CODY Plus, I never even really . . . come on, you probably heard the whole damn story.

MAN No, seriously, what? I mean, I knew you went off to school on some big scholarship, but that's all I—

CODY Right. (*Beat.*) Well, I . . . I hit a bad patch at college. Yeah. 'S what my ol' man called it. "A rough spot."

The MAN *doesn't seem in any hurry to get back to it, so* CODY *paces around. Thinking.*

CODY . . . I threw a race once, qualifying for nationals. This one race. Well, not *threw*, exactly, no, I guess I didn't "throw" it, 'cause to do that you'd have to lose, and I didn't. Nope. See, I won . . . won it, but I wasn't supposed to.

MAN Really. That's . . . So what was the, you know . . . ? I don't follow.

CODY . . . it was this . . . (*considers it*) . . . nothing. Forget it.

MAN No, what? Come on . . .

CODY *squats down near the* MAN *now, remembering.*

CODY . . . they wanted me to be a rabbit for 'em, my freshman year. And not even my event! I was done for the day with two firsts, but they asked me to take off quick in the five thousand and tire the other teams out, help our guys out— something to do with building my character and shit like that, *unity*—but I was like, "Fuck this," and took off running. Never looked back. I beat all 'a those motherfuckers. (*smiles*) Guess I'm not cut out for "team" sports . . . which I never knew track *was* till I got to college.

CODY *stops a second, recalling the moment. The* MAN *watches.*

CODY Anyways, I lost all my scholarships 'cause I would not apologize or back down. "Accept responsibility," I think they called it . . . and, you know, that's what folks wanna talk about in the end. To *dwell* on. Me being defiant. But my winning, they forgot all about that fact. Just like usual. People forget . . .
MAN Huh. Wow . . .
CODY Yeah, "wow" . . . and so that's what happened to the Olympics. That's as close as I ever got to any gold medal.

A long silence develops between the men—begrudging and respectful. These two may just be more alike than we first suspected.

After a moment, CODY *moves to the* MAN *and presses a finger into his chest.*

Neil LaBute

CODY . . . so, what's the next step?

MAN Whatever you want. Walk in on us at dinner or someplace . . . you decide.

CODY No, I thought you said that—

MAN Can we just play it by ear? I think it's gonna be better that way. More real . . .

CODY Yeah, fine. (*Beat.*) Just back off on the bigotry shit. Don't use that no more . . .

MAN I'm not a *racist*, would you stop! I did it for the effect . . . you're the one keeps bringing it up.

CODY I just don't want my kids hearing any of that.

MAN . . . Ralph is *two* . . .

CODY Cody Jr., then. I won't allow it.

MAN What the hell do you think I'd say? Huh?! I hardly saw 'em when I lived on your property, so . . . relax.

CODY It's hard enough out there, for a child like that.

MAN Like what?

CODY You know . . . he's . . .

MAN See? You're the one doing all the segregating . . . he's a little boy. He'll be fine! Parents break up all the time, and the children bounce back. That's-their-job. To bounce.

CODY Okay . . .

MAN . . . it is interesting, though, about the kids. Kids like yours. People always see you as these minorities, right, but then you look at their skin and all that—the children, I mean—and you guys're really the dominant ones. It's true. All the nappy hair and the big lips and shit . . . it always comes out on top, when your type gets together with some white girl. You ever notice that? I mean, not that anybody would *want* it, but it still does, all the same. Sure, they've got Belinda's eyes, but all the rest of it . . . 's straight from the *Congo.*

CODY is suddenly next to the MAN, right in his face. The MAN doesn't back off, and CODY lets him have it—pushes him hard on the chest, knocking him down. The MAN smiles, starts to get up, then dives at CODY's legs. He brings CODY down, and the two wrestle like a pair of Greco-Romans. It gets kind of nasty. (Actors are free to add their own assorted groans and fighting sounds here.) They finally release and move away. Exhausted.

The MAN stands up, wiping blood from his mouth with a tissue and moving down toward us. He glances back at CODY.

MAN All right, I admit it, that part was just a shameless attempt at a bit of action . . . little treat for the "gun and knife" crowd. But hey, you need to have something for everybody, right? I mean, take a look at the Elizabethans, you don't believe me. You give 'em the ol' soliloquy here, you have 'em grab their crotch over there . . . 'S all about *balance.* It is. In reality, he pushes me, I push back . . . you know, it's one of those *guy* fights. Lotta noise, not so much happens. (*Beat.*) Okay. So long as you know . . .

The MAN tucks his bloody tissue away and heads back to where CODY is sitting. Original tableaux—fancy name for same thing we just saw. After a long moment, CODY starts laughing. The MAN joins in.

CODY . . . you are a goofy fucker! Seriously. Just like back in school . . .

MAN We aim to please . . .

CODY Damn! I mean, shit, you're . . . crazy.

MAN Depends on the day, Mr. Phipps. On the day in
question . . .

CODY Yeah. But honestly, I don't want my kids hearing that . . .
stuff.

MAN I *understand* about the kids. And you want joint custody,
right?

CODY 'Course.

MAN Not total, because she'll never go for that. But we can try
to . . .

CODY Whatever we gotta do. Just do it.

MAN "Just do it." Nobody knows better than ol' Nike. She
was a goddess, wasn't she? In the ancient days, I mean.
Nike. I think that's where they got the, you know . . .
logo . . .

CODY Hell if I know. (*studying him*) You really are one odd
motherfucker . . .

MAN Thank you. Compliment accepted . . .

CODY Uh-huh. I need to go. Get myself off to work.

MAN Cool. I'm meeting Belinda later.

CODY Okay.

CODY *stops for a moment, then shakes his head. Laughs.*

CODY . . . man, that is just too strange. Being in on a thing like
that . . . *happy* she's cheating on me.

MAN We can stop. We can all go have us another *barbecue* if
you'd like.

CODY Funny. Real damn funny. Just do what you need to . . .

MAN I will.

CODY *nods and starts off, heading back toward town. The* MAN *stops him with a last question.*

MAN . . . what is it about her, though, Cody? That you hate so much?

CODY What?

MAN Just curious.

CODY I don't . . . (*Beat.*) No, I guess I do, actually. Hate 'er. Never thought of it that way, but yeah. I do.

MAN So . . . ?

CODY I dunno. After a while, it's a bit of everything, I s'pose. Her face, the way she flosses her teeth, all that stuff. Browsing my mail and shit. Yeah. I mean, it's great at first. She always looked real nice against my skin, walking around town hanging off my arm. I used to love it, I mean, it was *cool* . . . going over and waiting in her living room, to go out. With her parents standing there! (*Beat.*) And, yes, she is the mother of my kids and all, too, but after a while, you know . . . I guess the *novelty* of it just wore off.

MAN . . . that's nicely put. Succinct.

CODY Just trying to be honest.

MAN So, why didn't you, then? Why not just leave, or . . . ?

CODY 'Cause I got a place here in this community to think about. A legacy and the boys and all kinds 'a crap. She divorces me, and everybody says, "See, I told ya so. Told you it wouldn't work out," and they leave it at that. But if I go, if *I'm* the one to take off, well, then, I'm just some uppity black boy, got no business being here. My stores'll close, lose the house. Everything. (*Beat.*) The same reason my ol' man stayed . . . that guy hung in there, built his wife an empire. A goddamn *empire*! Dude weathered fuckin' El Niño

and you know what? The people *respected* him. They did.
They all understood he married a *cunt* and let it go at that . . .

MAN . . . but she's not at all like *your* mom, is she? Belinda, I
mean. No matter what kind of crap you've thrown at her, she
doesn't take off like your mother used to. Right? Hard as
you try . . .

CODY Don't. Do *not* . . .

MAN . . . which means she can never come crawling back, so
you can forgive her. Like your father used to.

CODY Dude . . . you just found yourself yet another topic to
keep your fucking *paws* off of. I mean it.

MAN It was just a guess . . .

CODY Yeah, well, suck my dick . . . piece 'a shit like you
talking about my *dad*.

MAN No, thanks. I only eat white meat.

CODY I can't wait till this thing is over.

MAN Me, too.

CODY Good.

MAN . . . 's a match made in heaven. She's making a point by
staying, and so are you! Wow. You two are—

CODY . . . I'm outta here . . . fuck you.

MAN You just keep your end of things up . . . I'll do the rest.
Have a nice day . . .

CODY *gives him the finger and walks off. Angry. The* MAN *turns
away and moves back down toward us. Sheepish grin.*

MAN . . . hey, sorry for that! Got a touch outta hand, so forgive
me. I should explain. You really need to take a good look at
the last few moments, decide for yourselves what happened
there. I mean, how much is real . . . (*Beat.*) It *happened*,

that much I can tell you. We did meet, talked for a bit, he gave me an envelope. We even ran. And I told you what went on—or will—when we get into our little shoving match. But the rest? Well, hey, that stuff's for you to decipher. I can't help you out with everything, wouldn't be any fun! But you guys had to be expecting at least one exchange like what you just saw, right? I mean, at *least* one . . . some swearing, the digs at women. A crazy plot twist. You had to know that something like that was gonna transpire! Without it, this would all be just so damn, what? I dunno. *Ordinary*, I guess. People in and out of love. Trouble breaks out. Happens all the time—movies, on the TV, your neighbors next door. And I'll tell you, it's not so outlandish, either, what just went on. Not with all that junk you see on the news. People, they tire of each other, give up on what they've got instead of fixing it, or trying to. It's easier to just . . . start over, go online, bury themselves at the office. *Any*thing rather than get to the bottom of their own shit. We're weak, that's really what it is. We are lazy and pushy and we want it all today. Or sooner, even. Now. And as long as we get it, our fair share— or even a pinch more—well, then, who really gives a fuck what happens to anybody else? Right?

The MAN *pulls that thick wad of cash out of his pocket, turns it over in his hands.*

MAN . . . this could be my deposit, what I gave them when I moved in. Maybe. Or it's a payoff for me to take the little missus off of Cody's hands. *Or* for that baseball card, even! Hell . . . this *might* just all be going through my head when I'm standing there at Sears, staring at Belinda again for the first time. I mean, don't look at me . . . I dunno where this damn thing is going, either! I really don't. All I do know is, whether any of that stuff you saw is real, the end result is this: I've started work on a play—it's *this* story, *technically*, but I've changed some of the situations around so that it's not . . . well, I don't think anybody's gonna notice. And especially not if it sells! (*Beat.*) Belinda is with me now, out of their house and living at my place. She's with the children most days, at least for the moment, just until they settle things, and Cody, well, he got what he wanted, too. He did. He finally got—after all those hurtful years of watching his dad take his mother back, time and time again—Cody got a white woman to walk out on him and stay gone. You should see him strutting around town now, telling anybody who'll listen about what Belinda did, and how hurtful it'll be on the kids and having the time of his life. How she never would've done this, something so humiliating to him, if he wasn't *black*. Seriously, people have told me he's said that very thing. "If I wasn't black." Yep, he's gone and pulled the ol' Ace 'a Spades out, one last time . . . wouldn't ya know it? (*Beat.*) Also, I think maybe I came off a little too, I dunno, *something*, in that last bit. Not like myself. "I can smell chick on you a mile away." I mean, come on! (*laughs*) But then, people are so many things, faces, in a given day, maybe that's just some side of me, this other part, that doesn't get out that often but is there. I dunno. But this time—'cause we're about to finish this off right now—this time out I'll be a bunch more like I was in the beginning. This is really about them now, anyhow, settling up and the like . . . I'm just there to be a support to her. To Belinda. Yep. I'm . . . anyway . . .

Things should probably change here to something more
formal—what the hell does that mean? I don't know. But we
could use a desk, maybe, and a few chairs. CODY *and the*
WOMAN *should already be seated, waiting. The* MAN *can wander*
over in his own time. Soon, but you know what I mean.

MAN . . . hello. Sorry that I'm . . .
WOMAN It's okay. (*checks* CODY) I mean, *fine.*
MAN Right, right . . . "fine but not okay." I remember.
WOMAN Yes. That's . . . right.

They sit in silence for a moment—make it a long one. CODY
glances around. Checks his watch.

CODY Where *is* this guy? (*to the* MAN) You see anybody out in
  the hall?
MAN Ahh, no, I didn't. I was just . . . no.
CODY Fine.
MAN I'm sure he's coming . . .
CODY Yeah? How do you know that?
MAN Just hopeful. That's all . . .
WOMAN Guys, let's not do this. Not right now . . . okay?

CODY *grunts and goes back to staring at the wall; the* MAN
reaches over and squeezes the WOMAN*'s hand. She smiles.*

CODY You two look over everything? The papers I had sent
  over, and the . . . ?
WOMAN Yes. (*looks directly at* CODY) You don't have to involve
  him, this is really between us.
CODY Hey, he's the one you're screwing now, so he can—

WOMAN I'm really not gonna sit here for that! I won't, Cody, I mean it.

CODY Fine. I'll shut up . . .

MAN . . . I doubt that . . .

CODY Fuck off.

MAN No, Cody, I don't want to. So I won't.

CODY *and the* MAN *have one of those adolescent male stare-downs;* CODY *blinks first. Looks away. Checks his watch again.*

CODY Two hundred bucks an hour, ya think he could be on *time* . . .

MAN Right.

WOMAN Yes. That'd be nice . . .

CODY Man . . . (*Beat.*) You did look at the stuff, though, right? I mean, all the changes from that last draft and the—

WOMAN Yes, Cody, we read it over. *Both* of us.

CODY Good. All right. And you're sure you want the single payment instead of the . . . ?

WOMAN Yes.

MAN We do. Yeah. Better to just finish this off, clean, and we can all . . . you agree to the custody schedule, and we're fine with the settlement. (*takes the* WOMAN's *hand*) We don't want your precious house or your stores, any of that crap. We'll manage . . .

CODY From what, your *book deals* . . . ?

WOMAN Cody . . .

CODY Just asking.

MAN I *don't* write books. I'm writing a . . . look, don't worry about us, okay?

CODY Whatever.

This Is How It Goes

MAN Seriously . . .

WOMAN We're going to be happy. That's what's important. Something *we* never figured out, you and me . . .

CODY That's bullshit, but think what you want.

WOMAN I will. I'm gonna think and feel and do whatever I want from now on. And you can't do anything about it. You can't yell at me, or make faces behind my back, or turn Cody Jr. against me anymore . . .

CODY Oh, *please* . . .

WOMAN You can't! You cannot do one damn thing to me . . . none of your silences or hitting or putting one of those dark fingers of yours anywhere near me. Not ever again. No, you are not *allowed* . . .

CODY . . . you better watch it . . .

MAN No, Cody, she doesn't have to . . .

CODY I said to watch your mouths, man!! BOTH OF YOU!! Just watch that kind of fucking shit around me . . .

CODY *stands up and slams his chair against the table, taking a step toward the* MAN. *The* MAN *remains seated, not engaging. That's probably best. The moment deflates, and* CODY *tries to save face—he heads for the door.*

CODY . . . I'm gonna go look in the hall, check on this motherfucker.

WOMAN You do that.

CODY I will.

MAN So, go then. Do it.

CODY *starts off, then looks back at the* MAN. *The* WOMAN, *too. A gleam in his eyes.*

Neil LaBute

CODY . . . but if I ever wanna trade back, you'll let me, right? Hmm?

The MAN *stares at him for a moment, then slowly nods;* CODY *smiles and exits. The* WOMAN *watches him go, looking at the door. The* MAN *watches, too, until the* WOMAN *turns to him.*

WOMAN . . . what's he mean by that?
MAN Oh, ya know.
WOMAN No, I don't. No. What?
MAN He's, ummm, he's just . . . Cody's just trying to . . .

They look at each other, then the WOMAN *glances at the door again. After a moment, the* MAN *rises and crosses to us.*

MAN Okay, sort of a dilemma here, right? Bit of a pickle . . . do I tell Belinda everything or make a run for it?

The MAN *glances back at her, then turns pleadingly to us for advice.*

MAN I'm serious, gimme some help here. I always imagined a day like this, one where she stumbles on to a cell-phone record or a scribbled note on a napkin and asks me about it . . . and I believe that I'd do the righteous thing. Tell her the truth. But the thing of it is, the truth is just so damn . . . elusive, isn't it? Like, I mean, *unknowable.* In the end. The second you start telling somebody what the truth is—how it goes—it all starts to slip away. Not, like, some lie, exactly, but close. This half-remembered version of one side 'a things. And what would the point be? I'll tell you this

This Is How It Goes

much—we end up pretty happy. Or will, however this time issue works itself out. We go and get married not too much later, even have ourselves a couple kids. Both boys, pleased to report. And we live happily ever after . . . or the equivalent of that, whatever that means today. Yes, we disagree on occasion, I sleep in the guest room every now and then, one of the kids breaks an eardrum when he's swimming, but all in all, we survive. We make it as a couple, and that, my friends, is not easy. It is work. But I love it, I do, I love her . . . always have. And I can see it on her face, at night or when we're on the back patio, at that blue hour when the sun's just dropped down . . . she is finally at peace. So what the hell am I gonna tell her right now to ruin it all? Huh? Nothing, that's what . . . I'm gonna make up some tale about a baseball card I've promised him from my collection and go with that. Stick with it to my dying breath . . . (*Beat.*) Quick story. The "Jackie Robinson" story. Cody gave me that card—it really is a nice one—if I'd go out with Belinda to the movies that one time. Time I mentioned way earlier. Remember? See, he was cheating on her, even way back then. He'd met this other girl, another cheerleader from over at Central, and he wanted to go out with her. That same night. So, he calls me, comes over, and tells me this whole tale about Belinda and how they're dating other people and shit and would I mind helping out? Cody tells me to go and pick her up at her house, six-thirty, and head over to the drive-in, this Showboat spot. He tells her the same thing— well, that I'm gonna pick her up, but—he'll meet us there, friends are joining us, I mean, the *usual* line of Cody Phipps bullshit. And that's how I end up seeing a movie with Belinda. One that she doesn't even remember going to. But I did get that card outta the deal. He was in a pinch, Cody was, and he agreed to it . . . screamed his head off, but yeah, he gave it to me. And this was the '52 Topps card with the red overlay. That thick smear of crimson on the backside—like a baboon's ass. Very scarce. But see, Cody was always so desperate to get into some white girl's pants that he'd part with something he really cared about. And that always made me hate him a bit—a little bit. Because he picked on me . . . picked me to help him, since I was no threat. Friendly and fat and always up for whatever. A perpetual Bachelor Number Two. I knew what he was doing, totally got it, but I liked her so much, Belinda, that I was willing to . . . anyway, that's the kind of guy Cody was. (*Beat.*) See, Cody Phipps was born a nigger. He still is, to this day. And I do know the difference, believe me, between regular black people and what Cody is. Oh yeah, absolutely. I never really liked the guy—yes, back in school, I'd hang with him, do some stuff, but basically just so he wouldn't make fun of me or knock me around. But Cody was always a nigger, even back then. This lazy, mean-spirited coon who acted like everybody owed him something. All that sort of post–Civil War, Malcolm X, heavy-lidded bullshit that guys like him've been trading on for years. Forty acres and a mule and always ready to lay down the ol' Ace 'a Spades. Well, hey, *man*, forgive us for dragging your sorry asses over here, 'cause-it-wasn't-fuckin'-worth-it!! (*Beat.*) Now, look . . . I don't really think in that way, use those terms very often, because the good side of me, the *educated* portion, says, "Hey, no, don't you do that, we're all God's chillun," and so on. But see, raised like I was, where I was—by *whom* I was— and that crap is always right up there, near the surface, waiting to bubble over. Cut me off in traffic sometime, you'll see what I mean! (*Beat.*) And anyhow . . . it's just a word, right? "Nigger." A word like any other. Only has power if you let it . . .

The MAN *looks back at the* WOMAN—*she's still staring off. Waiting for her cue. He looks back at us one more time.*

MAN But I'm not gonna screw this up . . . forget it. I'll make up a lie—I'm a lawyer, don't forget, *ex*, so it comes easy to me. Something. I'm not saying the other stuff was at all true, that crazy shit about us trading or whatever, but . . . we did see each other, Cody and I, at the airport that one time. And if she knows that, finds that out, then it's only another step to realize that Cody might've mentioned the garage apartment and some of their problems and all the rest. Maybe. And I'm not gonna take that chance, because from there it's only a hop-skip to understanding that, yes, I may have used this, used *them* in some way . . . to get what I wanted. What I've probably always wanted. Belinda. I'll tell ya one thing, though—whether he was in on it or not—Cody was no idiot. Not ever. He could see what I was up to—slowly trying to take her away, away from him—and he did nothing to stop me. *Encouraged* it, even. So, that says something . . . it does. I still see him, Cody, some days around town. Running. Over past the golf course and down there. I don't think there's so many hard feelings anymore. Least I hope not . . . (*He looks over at the* WOMAN.) But I'll smooth this over, and we can get on to all that stuff I just told you about. That good stuff. I can't wait . . . to be with her. Finally. After all this time. It's taken a lot to get here, to

Neil LaBute

this place, but it's all for the best, isn't it? Years of hatred and lies and betrayal that it took for Belinda and me to be together. For her to be happy. 'S worth it, though, right? Sure. I mean, *anything's* worth it, as long as you mean well . . .

The MAN *smiles at us, then returns to his seat next to the* WOMAN. *He takes her hand, and she turns back to him.*

WOMAN . . . what did he mean, sweetie?

MAN Nothing. It's a card, that's all. That stupid Jackie Robinson card he's been talking about . . .

WOMAN The rare one?

MAN Uh-huh.

A quiet falls over them as the WOMAN *studies the* MAN. *She reaches out and touches his face. Softly.*

WOMAN . . . I know what you've done.

MAN What? I mean—

WOMAN I do. I'm not stupid, so I know . . .

MAN I never said you were. (*Beat.*) Okay, honey, what? Come on, *what*?

WOMAN You gave it to him. Didn't you? That card.

MAN Ummm, well . . . yeah. Yes, I did.

WOMAN You felt bad, and you *gave* it to him . . .

MAN I . . . Look, I did it for you. For *us.* I thought it might, you know. Help. To smooth things over . . .

WOMAN Oh. (*Beat.*) So, what's he wanna give you for it? I thought you were . . .

MAN Just one of his players. His . . .

WOMAN Yeah?

MAN . . . yes. One of his good ones.

WOMAN Huh. You sure you want to? I mean, you love that thing
 . . . just don't let him *bully* you. Okay?

MAN I know. I won't.

WOMAN Because he can do that. Be a bully. And you've got a
 good heart, so . . .

MAN It's fine. (*smiles*) Promise.

WOMAN All right, then. (*Beat.*) You sure?

MAN No, yeah. I'm sure. Very sure. Yep. Very . . .

WOMAN . . . okay.

She smiles at the MAN, *then looks straight out at us. He
reaches over and kisses her on the cheek. Slowly turns out to
the audience. They are together now, but lost in their own
thoughts. Alone.*

Silence. Darkness.

Printed in the USA
CPSIA information can be obtained
at www.ICGtesting.com
LVHW091136150724
785511LV00001B/186